Foul Deeds and Suspicious Deaths in Guernsey

TRUE CRIME FROM WHARNCLIFFE

Foul Deeds and Suspicious Deaths Series

Barking, Dagenham & Chadwell Heath
Barnsley
Bath
Bedford
Birmingham
More Foul Deeds Birmingham
Black Country
Blackburn and Hyndburn
Bolton
Bradford
Brighton
Bristol
Cambridge
Carlisle
Chesterfield
Cumbria
More Foul Deeds Chesterfield
Colchester
Coventry
Croydon
Derby
Durham
Ealing
Fens
Folkstone and Dover
Grimsby
Guernsey
Guildford
Halifax
Hampstead, Holborn and St Pancras
Huddersfield
Hull
Jersey
Leeds
Leicester
Lewisham and Deptford
Liverpool
London's East End
London's West End
Manchester
Mansfield
More Foul Deeds Wakefield
Newcastle
Newport
Norfolk
Northampton
Nottingham
Oxfordshire
Pontefract and Castleford
Portsmouth
Rotherham
Scunthorpe
Southend-on-Sea
Southport
Staffordshire and the Potteries
Stratford and South Warwickshire
Tees
Warwickshire
Wigan
York

OTHER TRUE CRIME BOOKS FROM WHARNCLIFFE

A–Z of London Murders
A–Z of Yorkshire Murders
Black Barnsley
Brighton Crime and Vice 1800–2000
Durham Executions
Essex Murders
Executions & Hangings in Newcastle and Morpeth
Norfolk Mayhem and Murder
Norwich Murders
Strangeways Hanged
Unsolved Murders in Victorian & Edwardian London
Unsolved Norfolk Murders
Unsolved Yorkshire Murders
Warwickshire's Murderous Women
Yorkshire Hangmen
Yorkshire's Murderous Women

Foul Deeds & Suspicious Deaths in

GUERNSEY

Glynis Cooper

Series Editor

Brian Elliott

Wharncliffe Books

First published in Great Britain in 2006
and reprinted in 2012 by
Wharncliffe Local History
an imprint of
Pen & Sword Books Ltd
47 Church Street
Barnsley
South Yorkshire
S70 2AS

ISBN 978 1 84563 008 9

A CIP catalogue record for this book is
available from the British Library

Printed and bound in England
By CPI Group (UK) Ltd, Croydon, CR0 4YY

Pen & Sword Books Ltd incorporates the imprints of
Pen & Sword Aviation, Pen & Sword Family History, Pen & Sword Maritime,
Pen & Sword Military, Pen & Sword Discovery, Pen & Sword Politics,
Pen & Sword Atlas, Pen & Sword Archaeology, Wharncliffe Local History,
Wharncliffe True Crime, Wharncliffe Transport, Pen & Sword Select,
Pen & Sword Military Classics, Leo Cooper, The Praetorian Press,
Claymore Press, Remember When, Seaforth Publishing and Frontline Publishing

For a complete list of Pen & Sword titles please contact
PEN & SWORD BOOKS LIMITED
47 Church Street, Barnsley, South Yorkshire, S70 2AS, England.
E-mail: enquiries@pen-and-sword.co.uk
Website: www.pen-and-sword.co.uk

Contents

This book is dedicated to 'Our dear Channel Islands' (Winston Churchill, 1945); to my husband, Mike, who introduced me to the Islands; and to Colin, whose name means so much in Guernsey.

Acknowledgements

Grateful thanks are due to all those who helped in any way with this book and particularly the following: Amanda Bennett and the staff at the Priaulx Library in St Peter Port; Stephen Collas at the Guille Allès Library in St Peter Port; Alderney Museum; *Guernsey Press*, especially Di Digard for her unfailing encouragement and sense of humour; States Archive Service in St Peter Port; Rupert Harding of Pen & Sword Publishing for his help and support; Citizens Advice Bureau.

Introduction

The Channel Islands can sometimes seem a confusing place. They appear to be English: the people speak English; they talk of the English queen as their own queen; but they are not English. Neither are they a foreign country. They are officially regarded as an 'English Dominion' or a 'Crown Dependency' and Channel Islands matters are dealt with by the Home Office. However, the Islands are autonomous and the Home Office has no powers. Nor does the UK Parliament have any authority. The Islands are free to ignore Whitehall, except on matters of foreign policy, and they cannot declare war on another country without the permission of the British Foreign Office. They have their own legal system, their own government, their own taxation, their own stamp issue, their own unique royal blue post boxes and telephone kiosks, their own healthcare and social security systems. Though passports are not officially required by British people visiting the Islands, they are likely to be denied access to airlines and shipping lines without them. The currency is sterling but the Channel Islands have their own special notes and coins minted. British currency is legal on the Islands but Channel Islands currency is not legal tender in mainland Britain. The former currency was French francs and centimes; and before that the old Tours currency of livres, sols and deniers, better known as LSD, meaning – to those of a certain age in Britain – pounds, shillings and pence, not a hallucinatory drug.

Within the Channel Islands there are two separate Bailiwicks (from *bailie*, the French word for bailiff – and indeed the bailiwicks are still presided over by a Bailiff – and *wic*, Anglo-Saxon for village). The Bailiwicks are different areas of local government with some differing regulations. One comprises Jersey, the largest island of the group, Ecrehou, The Minquiers and Chausey; the other Guernsey, Alderney, Sark, and Herm, each with its own small 'off-island' of Lihou, Burhou, Brecqhou, and Jethou respectively. The Bailiwick of Jersey is closer to France and French was the official language of both Bailiwicks until 1926. The Islands lie off the coast of Normandy and the descent and traditions of the islanders are mostly Norman. However, Channel Islanders cling fiercely to the constitutional liberties granted to them by the English King John in 1204. After the Second World War, when the Islands were occupied by German forces for five years, the States (as the Islands are known) of Jersey and Alderney modernized their systems of government. Sark remains notoriously feudal. Guernsey did not update in the way that Jersey and Alderney have and the Guernsey constitution is a mixture of old and new, with regulations so confusing that even born and bred islanders cannot make sense of them.

Both Jersey and Guernsey are known for the richness of their milk and cream; their delicious new potatoes and ripe cherry tomatoes; and the thick-knit fishermen's sweaters to which both islands have given their name. In common with the rest of the group, the islands no longer rely on farming, fishing and smuggling for their livelihoods. Finance, construction and tourism have taken over. Even tiny Sark, with a population of just 600, has two banks and an avenue of gift shops. However, the Bailiwicks themselves are very separate and individual entities, and this book deals only with stories of foul deeds and suspicious deaths which occurred in the Bailiwick of Guernsey.

Guernsey has a steep and spectacular south coast (much painted by Renoir, the French Impressionist painter, in 1883),

Pleinmont Point and Hanois Lighthouse, showing Guernsey's treacherous south coast, *c.*1904. Author's collection

The west coast of Guernsey at Cobo, *c.*1908. Author's collection

which gazes out across the water to the other Channel Islands shimmering on the horizon; a wild and rocky west coast where huge harvest moons hang low in the sky; a mainly flat and sandy north coast where lie the remains of some of Europe's oldest settlements; and a shallow pretty east coast with the island's two main harbours of St Sampson and St Peter Port. The hinterlands are picturesquely rural with tranquil farms and villages. There are small cottages painted in brilliant white alongside stone nine-windowed farmhouses: two windows on each side of the front door and five windows across the first storey, the hallmark of houses built with money made from privateering and smuggling. Rounded Norman archways frame the front doors. In the seventeenth and eighteenth centuries the initials and the date of the wedding of a newly married couple would often be carved into the lintel, which became known as a marriage stone. Everywhere is very neat and very tidy as though a giant broom sweeps the island clean each morning.

Within the group Guernsey is an outlier, the Channel Island furthest from France and nearest to England. It is essentially an old Anglo-Norman island which still has strong feudal elements and it is important to understand the depth and sincerity of local belief in witchcraft, fairies, ancient forces, werewolves and the supernatural which has persisted right down to the twenty-first century. Fairies and werewolves have never been traditional features in the folklore of England. Although ancient Celtic customs, witchcraft and the supernatural played a strong part in English history (and still do in some parts of the country), the Industrial Revolution smashed a centuries-old way of life in England. That didn't happen on Guernsey. As late as 1914 the Royal Court could still believe that explaining someone's dream (an essential prerequisite for every modern psychologist) was witchcraft and that giving people little bags of blancmange powder to ease their headaches was an imprisonable offence.

Consequently any book on foul deeds and suspicious deaths in a place like Guernsey is not going to read like those which deal with similar incidents on the British mainland. Some of these deeds and deaths occurred on Guernsey simply because it was an island full of superstition and because ancient beliefs persisted for so long. In many ways it was an island apart, which the technological innovations of mainland Britain and the cultural sophistication of the Continent passed by. The west coast of Guernsey could be as remote as the Scottish Highlands and tourists on the modern buses have great difficulty in understanding that today's half-hour trip from St Peter Port to Pleinmont used to take two days in the eighteenth century. During the Second World War a German commanding officer unkindly referred to Guernsey folk as 'obsequious peasants'. His rudeness may have been sparked by an instinctive recognition of the feudal Norman mindset which has survived from the days of the Vikings to the Age of the New Technology, like the ancestral memory of Barbara Erskine's *Lady of Hay* and in Daphne du Maurier's novel, *The House on the Strand*. There is still much of the past in Guernsey's present, whether it is superstitious beliefs, feudal dues or the remnants of the terrific shock caused by the German Occupation (1940–45), and therefore it is the past which forms so much of the background and the theme of this book of true and often tragic stories.

With the exception of Chapters 17 ('Le Trepied') and 25 ('Island of Death'), there is a cut-off point of 1920 for the stories in this book. Guernsey is still a small place and many families are well known and inter-related. The aim of this book is to chronicle in entertaining form foul and dastardly deeds, murders and suspicious deaths which have occurred within the Bailiwick; not to embarrass those still living who may have memories which they would rather forget. The case of 'Island of Death' is different because there were no local people living on Alderney when the incidents described took place and because they form an integral and unique part of island history; a history which is not yet fully recorded in the public domain. Chapter 17, 'Le Trepied', set on Guernsey's romantic west coast is, to quote the title of a well-known television series, strange but true.

CHAPTER 1

A Brief History of the Guernsey Bailiwick

Guernsey has not always been an island. During the last Ice Age, ten thousand years ago, Guernsey and Herm were joined together as a single island and there was a land bridge linking this island to Alderney and from there to the French mainland. As the ice melted and sea levels rose the land links were severed. Guernsey and Herm, however, have only been separated for a millennium or more. The pattern is similar to what happened with the Isles of Scilly which lie off Cornwall; and like the Isles of Scilly, Guernsey too is still a drowning land. That much is obvious at low tide on the west coast where the naked eye can easily pick out the original shorelines at Rocquaine, Perelle, Vazon and Cobo. Around Vazon submerged peat remains indicate the remnants of woodlands near Fort Hommet and the prehistoric farm site at Albecq.

The settlers on the west coast were not the earliest settlers. Les Fouaillages at L'Ancresse in the north of the island belonged to the Mesolithic hunter-gatherers of 5000 BC before being settled later by Neolithic farming folk. Later Les Fouaillages became a ritual and burial site for over 2,500 years before reverting to farming use, for which the fertile ground that lay on the edge of alder, elm, oak and hazel woodlands was ideal. These later inhabitants left behind their pottery, loom weights and arrowheads. The Channel Islands formed part of the ritual landscape which covered Western Europe during the late Neolithic period and the Bronze Age. This landscape was characterized by stone circles, menhirs, dolmens, cursii (earthen banks linking ritual features), cairns, and sometimes ritual hearths. The best example of a dolmen on Guernsey is the passage grave at Le Déhus near Bordeaux in Vale. There is a 'Guardian' figure carved on one of the capstones. At Les Fouaillages a house of the dead was built among the earlier tombs around 2500 BC. Seven hundred years later the Beaker People (named after the distinctive pottery drinking beakers which they made) arrived from the Iberian Peninsula (probably from the area now known as Portugal).

There is shipwreck and amphorae evidence that 2,000 years later there was still a trading connection with the Iberian Peninsula. L'Ancresse Common, together with its rich inheritance of prehistoric features, was covered with blown sand sometime during the 800s, a period when the weather was so exceptionally stormy that Hugh Dorndighe, an early ninth-century Irish king, wrote of it in his diary.

However it was the Iron Age Celts who made the biggest impact on Guernsey, and their influence still survives today. Although their culture (in two phases known as Hallstatt and La Tène) is said to have originated in the Austrian salt-mining villages during the seventh century BC, the people were the descendants of a migration which had begun around 1000 BC in south-west Anatolia (modern Turkey) and swept northwards and westwards across Europe. Today there are said to be five remaining Celtic kingdoms: Wales, Scotland, Ireland, Cornwall and Britanny. Britanny lies adjacent to Normandy on the western coast of France and is little further away from the Channel Islands than the Scillies are from Cornwall. Islands held a fascination for the Celts, who revered water, and sometimes in Celtic mythology the Celtic 'otherworld' has been described as 'the islands far across and sometimes under the Western ocean'. Drowning islands: a description which fits the Isles of Scilly as

'The Guardian' of Le Déhus dolmen, *c.*1910. Author's collection

La Roque qui Sonne, *c.*1950. Standing stone in St Sampson – a menhir which characterized the ritual landscape of Bronze Age Guernsey.
Reproduced by kind permission of the Priaulx Library, St Peter Port, Guernsey

well as the Channel Islands, and indeed the two groups of islands have much Celtic folklore in common.

The Celts were a passionate, vibrant, artistic people who brought their iron-working skills to Guernsey with them. There are several Celtic (or Iron Age) sites on the island. They worshipped a mother goddess, believing the mother to be the giver of life, and the 'trinity of fertility' (birth, death, rebirth) based on the agricultural calendar. Their main festivals were: Imbolc (Festival of the Lambs on 1 February); Beltane (May Day, 1 May); Lughnasadh (Harvest Thanksgiving on 1 August); and Samhain (Old Year's Eve, 31 October; their New Year's Day being 1 November). There are two 'statue menhirs' of the mother goddess on Guernsey; each some 1.5 metres tall. One stands at the lych gate to St Martins' Church; the other in Câstel churchyard. There are three phases to the Celtic mother goddess: maiden (innocence); mother (fruitful bearer of children); hag (old 'wise woman'). Though damaged by over-zealous Christian ministers in past centuries, the prominence of the breasts on the statues probably indicates that they represented the second phase, of the mother. It was customary to leave 'offerings' at the 'mother's' feet. Even today, at the old Celtic festival of Beltane, bunches of flowers are laid at the feet of both mother goddess statues and sometimes garlands of flowers are placed on their heads. In 1921 Lieutenant Colonel T W M de Guerin drew up a list of over 150 dolmens, menhirs, sacred rocks and holy wells which still existed scattered around Guernsey. Offerings were, and in some cases still are, placed beside many of them on certain days of the year.

There was an unusually strong belief in witchcraft (see Chapter 13, 'Bewitching Guernsey') on the island which persisted until at least the Second World War. Guernsey folk were terrified to an astonishing degree of being bewitched, of spells being placed on them, of having the 'evil eye' cast upon them. In fact the last witchcraft trial in Guernsey took place on the eve of the First World War in 1914 (Chapter 18, 'The Magic of Brown & Polson'). It could be said perhaps that the idea of a witch was originally derived from the Celtic 'hag', the 'wise woman' who had a way with herbs and healing often thought to be magical. There was also a very strong tradition of the Devil in Guernsey and he was more often than not associated with the witches. The Devil was apparently also given to appearing in animal form: as a goat or as a werewolf (Chapter 7, 'Call of the Werewolf'), or, most commonly,

La Gran'mère du Chimquière, mother goddess statue dating from *c.*2200 BC which today stands by the lych gate of the parish church in St Martins. On May Day she is garlanded and offerings are placed at her feet. The author

Menhir representing prehistoric Mother Goddess of the 'Old Golden Land'. Flowers at her feet show she is still revered today. The author

as a large black dog which became known as the 'dog of death'. This last ties in with the legend of Black Shuck, common in the West Country and East Anglia.

There was, too, a great belief in fairies, 'the little people', in Guernsey – a kind of hybrid of the 'little people' of Ireland and the Cornish pixies. As anyone who has ever read fairy stories knows, fairies are usually the 'good guys', with certain exceptions like the bad fairy at Sleeping Beauty's christening; but in Guernsey the fairies were a very mixed bunch. They could be selfish, cruel and vindictive as well as kind, charming and helpful. Many fairies were believed to be 'foreign fairies' who had a king named Colin and who entered Guernsey via a dolmen known as Le Creux es Faies at L'Erée, not far from Fort Saumarez similarly named, and through a cave at Vazon. The home of these 'foreign fairies' was said to be across the sea in England, ironically the one country of the British Isles which does not have a particularly strong fairy tradition.

Tower Hill, *c.*1960, the former site of the witch burnings in St Peter Port, now built up and part of the modern town centre. Reproduced by kind permission of the Priaulx Library, St Peter Port, Guernsey

The origins of the name Guernsey are obscure. However, the suffix *-ey* (Guernsey, Jersey, Alderney) comes from the Norse *-oy*, which means 'island'; and *-hou* (Lihou, Ecrehou, Burhou, Brecqhou, Jethou) is derived from the Norse *holm*, which means 'islet'. There are ten parishes on Guernsey, and (unlike Jersey parishes) three are split and one has no coastline. St Pierre du Bois, Torteval and Vale are split. St Andrew has no coastline. The other parishes are: St Peter Port, St Martins, Câstel, Forest, St Sampson and St Saviour. Today Guernsey has a population of around 60,000 people and there are about 70,000 vehicles, which is amazing on an island measuring only 18 kilometres long by 7 kilometres wide.

Bretons, Celts from Brittany, inhabited Guernsey until the time of the Viking raids in the eighth to tenth centuries. The Norsemen were wild and fierce and caused a good deal of grief to the Channel Islands. In 911 Charles the Simple of France, thoroughly fed up with the repeated attacks of one particular Viking chief named Rollo, drew up a treaty giving Rollo the province of Normandy and creating him Duke of Normandy in return for Rollo's promise to keep the peace. When Rollo died in 929, his son, William Longsword, became Duke of Normandy and he annexed the Channel Islands in 933. It was the Vikings who laid down the basis of feudalism in the Islands and in the tenth century this worked well. Over a century later, in 1066, William, Duke of Normandy, invaded England and conquered the country, earning himself the title of William the Conqueror for posterity. Through William the Channel Islands and England were then united under one king.

The king made grants of land in the Channel Islands, called fiefs, to his favourite nobility in return for military services. Each fief was held by a Seigneur whose home was the manor house. All the other inhabitants of a fief were the Seigneur's tenants, even if they owned their own homes. Each tenant generally paid his rent in foodstuffs (grain, eggs, meat, and so on). The bigger fiefs had their own corn-grinding mills which the tenants were obliged to use. Feudal courts were called Courts of Chief Pleas (and still are on Sark) and were held on each fief. Stone seats used by these courts can still be seen on some of the fiefs.

Today the Royal Court in Guernsey sits three times a year as a Court of Chief Pleas. It is presided over by the Bailiff of the Island and twelve Jurats (who are elected for life); and the Seigneurs, advocates (lawyers) and police constables of each parish must attend. Guernsey also clings to another ancient Norman custom that is regarded as nothing short of quaint and eccentric in the twenty-first century. If someone feels that his or her property or rights are being infringed by another person, he or she can invoke the 'Clameur de Haro' and in 'the presence of two witnesses he or she must kneel and cry "Haro! Haro! Haro! à l'aide mon prince! on me fait tort!" and then he or she has to recite the Lord's Prayer in French'. The disputed property or right is then 'under the protection of the Queen and a court case must be brought within a year and a day' (Peter Johnston, *A Short History of Guernsey*).

King John was not the most able or popular of English kings. He was the bad King John of Robin Hood legend who ill-treated his subjects, he lost the Crown Jewels in marshes off the Wash on the Norfolk coast, and he pestered the life out of 'Maid Marian'. John, by rights, should not have been king, but his older and more able brother, Richard Coeur de Lion, was away for most of the time fighting in the Crusades, and John found himself as a sort of king-regent. In 1204 he lost Normandy to the French, which left the Channel Islands in the front line. John, anxious to retain the Islands as a base from which to attack France, offered the islanders generous terms to remain loyal to the English Crown.

After due consideration they agreed and have remained so ever since. Castle Cornet in St Peter Port was built in 1204 to defend Guernsey, and was joined shortly afterwards by Vale Castle in St Sampson and the nearby Château des Marais, but for almost three hundred years afterwards the island (along with its sister isles) suffered badly, mostly from raids by the French, until in 1480 Pope Sixtus IV issued a Papal Bull granting all the Channel Islands the 'Privilege of Neutrality'. During this same period pirates also made a considerable nuisance of themselves in the Guernsey Bailiwick, especially on Sark, which was depopulated for a time, and, with its almost inaccessible cliffs, offered pirates a safe haven until a surprise French invasion in 1549.

During the Middle Ages there were a number of small chapels established on Guernsey, though the only one to survive intact is that of St Apolline (patron saint of dentists) in St Saviour's parish. Most of the monastic establishments on Guernsey were under the Abbey of the romantic Mont-Saint-Michel until the Confiscation of Alien Priories by Henry V in 1416. Before the Reformation much of Guernsey's spiritual welfare had been supervised by the See of Coutances in Normandy, the Bishop there receiving feudal dues from the Guernsey churches. In 1568 Elizabeth I put a stop

Gathering 'vraic' (seaweed) near Vale, 1905. Author's collection

to that and placed Guernsey and the rest of the Islands within the diocese of Winchester. Against her better judgement she also allowed Calvin's doctrine of Presbyterianism to flourish on Guernsey in order to (in modern idiom) 'keep the islanders sweet'. In 1563 the Queen had founded Elizabeth College in St Peter Port as a grammar school and she hoped that by providing decent education on the island it would lessen the Calvinist influences to which scholars were subject in French schools. French was then the official language of the Islands and Guernsey's better-off sons were educated in France prior to 1563.

Given this and Guernsey's ancient sworn oath of loyalty to the English Crown, it came as quite a surprise that just three generations later Guernsey turned against the Crown during the English Civil War (1640–49) and came out on the side of the Parliamentarians. This was partly due to dislike and mistrust of Sir Thomas Leighton, the extremely unpopular, if very efficient and effective, Crown Administrator for Guernsey from 1570 to 1610; and partly due to Charles I's heavy-handed methods in dealing with Guernsey, appointing an unsympathetic governor in the person of Sir Peter Osborne, and billeting a large number of troops on the island while refusing to pay for their upkeep. Although Sir Peter held Castle Cornet for the Royalists, the rest of Guernsey supported Cromwell. Jersey, which had remained loyal to the king and was contemptuous of its sister isle, supplied the Castle and allowed it to hold out for nearly nine years. Records show that 30,000 cannon balls were fired from the Castle into St Peter Port during the Civil War, so that the old town was virtually completely destroyed.

During the Civil War several attempts were made to turn the tide and bring Guernsey into the Royalist camp. These included kidnapping three Parliamentary Commissioners who were imprisoned in Castle Cornet to await execution. Their story is told in Chapter 16 ('Escape from Death'). In 1660 however, two years after Cromwell's death, the monarchy was restored, albeit with greatly reduced powers. Parliament, and not the Sovereign, now ruled the country. This placed Guernsey in something of an awkward position. The island owed allegiance to the king, as it had done since Norman times, but not to Parliament. However, by supporting Parliament during the Civil War Guernsey found itself in a kind of 'no man's land', with all the island's ancient rights and privileges at stake. Some of the island's leading families, who had remained loyal to the monarchy, therefore took a petition to Charles II acknowledging that the island had been wrong in its actions during the war and pleading for a royal pardon. The king, wishing to be seen as gracious and benevolent in his restoration, no matter what his private feelings were, granted the pardon and restored Guernsey's rights and privileges.

Just over ten years later there occurred what insurance companies term 'an act of God', a remarkable occurrence which must have caused the superstitious islanders to wonder just how much they had displeased their higher authority. On New Year's Eve 1672 there was a violent thunderstorm and lightning struck the 'donjon' (central tower) in which all the gunpowder was stored. There was an enormous explosion which completely destroyed the tower, the chapel, the banqueting hall and the Governor's residence. Several people were killed, including the Governor's wife, mother and daughter. The Governor himself, Sir Christopher Hatton, had gone to bed later than his wife and, not wishing to disturb her, decided to sleep in one of the dressing rooms. When he woke up after the explosion he was still lying in his bed, and uninjured, but the bed had been blown onto the battlements.

The two hundred years following the Restoration were years of enormous prosperity for Guernsey. The island supplemented its traditional occupations of farming and fishing with smuggling, or 'free trade' as it was known (Chapter 5, 'Watch the Wall My Darling') and privateering (Chapter 10, 'Daylight Robbery'). Subsidiary industries were spawned from these activities. At one time as many as six hundred coopers were employed on the island making barrels for wine and brandy for the 'free trade'. There were also several shipbuilding yards to cater for the demand for ships at the height of the privateering era. Privateer ships (that is ships privately built and owned by one family or a group of families) had royal letters of permission on royal headed notepaper (Letters of Marque) to attack any enemy shipping. Though the Hanoverian monarchs had specified France (still looking to attack the Channel Islands) and Spain and their allies as the specific enemies of the British Crown, many of the privateers took these letters as carte blanche to attack whomsoever they pleased. When George III protested and took them to task the privateers began to attack English shipping as well. A number of Guernsey families became extremely wealthy and several of the island's larger houses and the Georgian houses in St Peter Port were built from the millions of pounds brought into the island through privateering and 'free trade'. In 1777 the Assembly Rooms and the covered market were built (in 1787 John Wesley came to St Peter Port and preached in the Assembly Rooms prior to the introduction of Methodism to Guernsey). The market still exists as a market, but the Assembly Rooms became the Guille Allès library in 1870, taking its name from its benefactors.

It was towards the end of the eighteenth century that Guernsey began to become a fortified island. A Guernsey Militia had existed for several hundred years, but its members did not have to serve away from the island, thanks to privileges granted by King John, 'except to restore the king to his throne or to rescue him from a foreign prison' (Peter Johnston, *A Short History of Guernsey*), though this must have rung a little hollow after the debacle of the Civil War. Between 1775 and 1790 fifteen coastal defence towers were built around Guernsey's coast. Fort George was begun in 1782 and took thirty years to complete. The French Revolution of 1789 unnerved everyone, and because of the threat from the Revolutionaries and, later, Napoleon, another sixteen forts and fifty-eight coastal batteries had been added by 1815 to the defences already in place around the island's coastline. A planned attack by the French in 1794 was foiled because of the state of 'red alert' on all the Islands and the successful naval defence action off the west coast of Guernsey by one of the island's greatest heroes, Captain James Saumarez, later Admiral Lord de Saumarez and Vice-Admiral of Britain in 1821. Numerous regiments were brought in and stationed on the island to staff the fortifications; but there was little for the soldiers to do in their off-duty time and this led to boredom, heavy drinking (see Chapter 22, 'Ghost of the Murdered') and crime (Chapter 28, 'Pictures on a Gravestone').

Until 1806 mainland Guernsey was actually two islands. The Clos du Valle in Vale in the north of the island was separated by the Braye du Valle, a channel which ran from Grande Havre on the west coast to St Sampson Bridge on the east coast. At low tide it was possible to cross by means of two causeways near the church of St Michel du Valle in Vale in the west and two crossings further to the east near the Bailloterie and the Tertre. The Braye was drained to stop the French sailing up to attack. Salt 'wiches' that lay along the edge of the Braye were lost when it was drained. All that is left to show the path of the original tidal channel is Vale Pond near the church. The reclaimed land was sold and the money used to improve the terrible state of the road, much to the annoyance of Guernsey folk who argued that the bad roads would act as a deterrent to the French. A more likely reason, however, was that maintaining good roads meant increasing taxes and despite the wealth of a number of people, taxation, then as now, was anathema to them.

The ordinary country folk on Guernsey lived in quite a

different manner to their wealthier counterparts. Most cottages were small and quite dark with thick walls to keep out the incessant winds that howl around the islands. Downstairs living rooms had bare earthen floors which were sanded and called a 'Vale carpet'. The 'Vale carpet' was usually covered with bracken, which required changing quite frequently. Furniture tended to be basic, consisting of chairs and a table and perhaps a kind of kitchen dresser. However, every house had its 'green bed', which was a narrow single bed about half a metre high, of dry ferns, which usually stood against the wall near the fire. This was the

Fountain Street, St Peter Port, gives an idea of how the older, poorer part of the town would have looked in the nineteenth century. Reproduced by kind permission of the Priaulx Library, St Peter Port, Guernsey

Cornet Street in St Peter Port as Victor Hugo would have known it.
Reproduced by kind permission of the Priaulx Library, St Peter Port, Guernsey

poor person's version of a settee but they were quite comfortable. Peat, brushwood, cowpats and seaweed were used for the fire and must have given off a pungent fragrance. At night the room was lit by a fish-oil lamp called a crâsset. Bad roads and lack of transport meant that many never left their own parishes. G B Edwards' novel *The Book of Ebenezer Le Page* gives an excellent picture of life in rural Guernsey before the Second World War.

One of the most famous people to live on the island was not a Guernseyman at all. The renowned novelist, Victor Hugo, left his native France in 1851 as a political refugee from the regime of Louis Napoleon. He settled in Jersey, where his outspokenness landed him in trouble once more, and he was expelled from the island in 1855 for criticizing a state visit to Paris made by Queen Victoria. On Hallowe'en 1855 he arrived in Guernsey, which was to be his home for the next fifteen years. He bought Hauteville House in St Peter Port for himself, his wife 'la mère de mes enfants', and his family, including his son François Victor; and a few doors down the road he installed 'mon ami' Juliette Drouet, his mistress for many years. Most of Hauteville House was dark and sombre but Hugo had his study on the top floor, which was

Bottom of Cornet Street, *c.*1910 (showing Town Church). St Peter Port had expanded to accommodate growing trade and an increasing number of itinerant workers. Reproduced by kind permission of the Priaulx Library, St Peter Port, Guernsey

light and bright with a view of the sea. He always wrote standing up, leaning on a lectern-style desk while he penned his masterpieces. It was here in this room that he wrote *Les Misérables*, *Les Travailleurs de la mer* and *L'Homme qui rit*. The haunted house featured by Hugo in *Les Travailleurs de la mer* was based on a small watch-house which stood between Les Tielles Battery and Mont Herault on Guernsey's south coast. This particular house no longer exists but the watch-house at Mont Herault is very similar. In 1870 Victor Hugo finally returned to France and in 1885 a commemorative statue to him was erected in Candie Gardens.

The expansion of the nineteenth and early twentieth centuries brought many itinerant workers to Guernsey, attracted by jobs in the construction and quarrying industries, and this brought its own problems, with workers far from home taking lodgings, growing disenchanted, and generally 'losing the plot' (see Chapter 4 'A French Tragedy' and Chapter 21, 'How Did She Die?'). However, the main event of the twentieth century, which shook Guernsey to its very roots, was the German occupation of the island from 1940 to 1945. Hitler was keen for the occupation of the Channel Islands to be a 'model occupation', to show that life under the Nazis would be all right and that providing everyone did as they were told everything would be fine and there would be no problems; but men and women were designed to be free agents and Hitler badly misjudged the human spirit.

Channel Islanders often feel misunderstood about the role they played during the Occupation and they are defensive, saying 'You weren't here, you don't know what it was like.' This is perfectly true and it is difficult to say how one would react in such circumstances. However, Poland, France and Holland suffered a much more brutal occupation but they were renowned for their fierce resistance movements. Although one cannot accuse the Channel Islanders of much active collaboration, neither was there much active resistance.

The Occupation was a defining moment in history for Guernsey. All the Channel Islands were occupied by the German forces but it was Guernsey which seemed to suffer the most profound shock and showed at least some of the island's population in an extremely unfavourable light. When Churchill's government took the decision to demilitarize 'our dear Channel Islands' in 1940, many of the islanders could be forgiven for thinking they were being abandoned. In this belief they were supported by a fair number of people, including some in the Government. Their belief was strengthened when the Government announced that it was impractical and impossible to evacuate everyone in the Islands, and that children, mothers of young children and young men of military service age were to be given priority. The Bailiff and administration on Guernsey dithered while rumours and misinformation abounded on the island, causing general panic and confusion. The other Channel Islands had better leadership. The Dame of Sark firmly announced that none of the Sarkese would be leaving, while Judge French on Alderney took the opposite decision and announced that the entire population of 1,800 would be evacuating the island. On Jersey, the Bailiff, Alexander Coutanche, did his best to be reassuring and stated that there was no need for panic or a mass evacuation. Churchill reassured the islanders that demilitarization was for their own safety to prevent German attacks. This reassurance rang rather hollow when German bombers strafed the quay in St Peter Port just before the Occupation in the mistaken belief that trucks loading tomatoes for export were troop carriers. Thirty-four islanders died.

It was at this point that some Guernsey folk began to show themselves in a less than favourable light. Families who had decided to leave the island arrived at the quay to find insufficient ships, with people crammed into every available space on board. Knowing that there would be no military escort, many decided the risk just wasn't worth it, changed their minds about evacuating to England, and returned home to find their houses already stripped bare. Such looting continued after the German forces arrived, and it was a bitter pill for Guernsey people to swallow when it was discovered that it was not the occupying force who were responsible and that the culprits included a number of their own policemen. Guernseymen were also responsible for pillaging homes on Alderney (see Chapter 25, 'The Island of Death') after the inhabitants had left and seven local people were imprisoned by the Royal Court as a result. (See Peter Tabb, *A Peculiar Occupation*, pp. 134–5; Madeleine Bunting, *A Model Occupation*, pp. 34–5, 137 and 264–5.)

Worse was to come. On Jersey the islanders had decided on a policy of being distantly polite to the Germans, in the interests of self-preservation, while at the same time being passively resistant. As Hitler issued more edicts against the Jews and insisted upon their implementation, the Jersey administration questioned the registration of the Jews and did no more than was asked of them. The Germans harassed some of the Jews on Jersey but none of them, so far as is known, were sent to the gas chambers of the concentration camps, and one Jewish girl was successfully hidden in St Helier for the last two years of the war. On Guernsey it appears that officials were more willing to co-operate with the occupying forces than on Jersey and to hand over the few Jews who were on the island. One Jewish woman, working hard and keeping a low profile on a Guernsey farm, was betrayed by an island informer. Another had been trapped in the Islands at the outbreak of war when she was on holiday on Sark with her employers. A third worked as a hospital cleaner. These three Jewish women were handed over to the Germans by the Guernsey police in July 1942 and deported to Auschwitz. Less than a week later they were dead. The extent of collaboration between islanders and the occupying forces has caused some bitterness between the two islands. (See Madeleine Bunting, *A Model Occupation*, pp. 105–14, especially p. 111; Guernsey State Archives for 1942; Paul Sanders, *The British Channel Islands under German Occupation*, pp. 133–43; Peter Tabb, *A Peculiar Occupation*.)

Although the States Archives on Guernsey hold a number of war records and Feldkommandant's papers, full understanding of the Occupation history of Guernsey is hampered by the withholding and embargo until 2045 of some of the Guernsey war files

St Peter Port on Guernsey shortly after the Occupation (1940–45) had ended. The bus station now stands where the avenue of trees can be seen close to the shore. Author's collection

by the British Government. Most of Alderney's wartime records have similar restrictions, despite efforts by some MPs in 1992 to have all Channel Islands war records released. Some reports suggest that Churchill was less than pleased by the Islands' conduct throughout the war, but then Churchill was not living under constant threat in occupied territory. After D-Day in 1944 and the Allies had recaptured Normandy from the Germans, supplies of food, clothing, medicines and fuel to the Islands ceased. By Christmas that year islanders were close to either starvation or dying from hypothermia. Churchill was determined that the German troops should not receive any supplies but it may also have been a measure of his feelings about the islanders that he took so long to allow the Red Cross ship *Vega* to bring food and medical supplies for them. The ship finally arrived from Lisbon on 27 December and then made monthly visits until the liberation of the Islands in May 1945.

Liberation was a mixed blessing. Alderney had been ruined by the prison camps, the sheer number of slave workers, and the Nazi SS (see Chapter 25, 'The Island of Death'). Sark probably escaped most lightly, owing to its small size and the steep rocky coastline providing natural defences. In fact Sark was not liberated until 10 May, the day after Guernsey. Herm was too small to have been of much interest to the Germans or to anyone else. Guernsey was left with a wealth of ugly concrete bunkers, gun emplacements, fortifications (often built over pre-existing ones from the Napoleonic era) and signal stations. The island was also left with a legacy of bitterness caused by the looting of evacuated islanders' houses, informants, collaborators and 'jerry bags', the islanders' term for girls who fraternized with the Germans. Every year on 9 May Guernsey stages Liberation Day celebrations. The sixtieth anniversary was in 2005 and the island put on a glittering show. Though many islanders are ambivalent in their feelings towards England and the English, they requested the presence of the Queen at the celebrations. She came, wearing red, the colour of life. Watching the splendid parades and the semblance of unity, there is a feeling that Guernsey has rewritten this part of its history. The Occupation will dominate islanders' lives for years, possibly generations, to come, and the island has to come to terms with what happened.

On the surface, that has happened. Guernsey is a rich and thriving island once again, thanks to tourism and to the finance industry, attracted by its liberal tax laws. Chrome and glass edifices have replaced humble cottages and wartime ruins. Fashion shops and gift shops, banks and jewellers fill the town centre. There is no VAT to pay on anything. Alcohol is cheaper than in mainland Britain, dearer than in France. House prices are booming. The island looks clean and affluent and shining. Underneath the surface, however, suspicions still lurk and superstitions are still strong. Guernsey folk do not want to talk about the past. They are wary of outsiders and nervous of change; and in some there are still traces of the Norman settlers of 1,000 years ago.

CHAPTER 2

A Foul and Dastardly Murder and Execution

1854

'She had been burned while she was alive and conscious and she had died in convulsive agony.'

Although the death penalty was not repealed in Guernsey until 1965, the last execution for murder took place over a century before, in 1854. The main reason for this was that the execution went badly wrong and the manner of the murderer's death was almost as dreadful as that of his victim. For an island used to grisly executions such as the burning alive of pregnant witches, the slow garrotting of pirates, and agonizing deaths of those who died from 'divers tortures' in Castle Cornet, that was quite an achievement. The whole story makes for horribly gruesome reading and illustrates the appalling inhumanity that man is capable of towards both man and woman.

John Charles Tapner worked as a clerk in the Engineers' department at Fort George on the edge of St Peter Port in Guernsey. He was thirty years old, with a penchant for living beyond his means, a reputation as a petty thief and a complicated love life. He married a lady named Mary Gahagan in the late 1840s and made a home with her and their three sons at Villa de La Roche in St Martins. However, he later began an affair with her sister, Margaret Gahagan. They had an illegitimate baby and Tapner stayed some of the time with Margaret in the Canichers. He quickly discovered 'what tangled webs we weave when first we practise to deceive' and the cost of those tangled webs. His money problems became even more pressing. He was constantly in debt and constantly in need of ever more money to fund his chosen lifestyle.

However, while living in the Canichers it came to his notice that one of his neighbours, Elizabeth Saujon, a seventy-four-year-old widow, kept substantial sums of cash and several items of value in her house. She sometimes took in lodgers to supplement her income and so Tapner did his homework on what he had heard and lodged with her for about ten days. This told him all he needed to know about her possessions and her domestic habits. It would be so easy, he thought, and after all he didn't see that she really needed all that cash. If it had just been a simple robbery that he planned it would have gone largely unremarked; but there was a darker side to John Tapner's nature.

On 18 October 1853 Mary de Jersey left the house of her friend, Elizabeth Saujon, at about nine o'clock in the evening. Soon after she had left, a man with a walking stick entered Elizabeth's house through the front door, which was always left unlocked. Elizabeth recognized her visitor as the man who had lodged with her previously and chatted to him companionably. Perhaps she offered him some tea and turned away to put the kettle on. Perhaps she turned to fetch something. That will never be known. What is known is that as she did so the man brought the walking stick down on her head with such force that the blow split her head open, dented her skull, and left a fracture above her right ear where she had been hit. She collapsed immediately. While Elizabeth lay helpless and unconscious on the floor, the man ransacked her home, taking anything he felt was of value, money, her jewellery. He even took her wedding ring. He then dragged her into her bedroom, dousing her body and the room with turpentine, before fastening the doors and shutters, lighting a match and making good his escape.

Next day Elizabeth's neighbour, Robert Hutton, became concerned that her shutters were still closed at noon. He knocked on her door and when he received no answer he went to fetch PC James Barbet. They and another neighbour, Joshua Ahier, tried to get into the house but they did not succeed, so PC Barbet sent for a ladder and Joshua Ahier finally gained entry through an upstairs window. He discovered the living room and Elizabeth's bedroom still full of dark choking smoke and her charred body lying on her bedroom floor with her hands clenched on her chest. An autopsy revealed that the blow to her head had not killed her. She had been burned while she was alive and conscious and she had died in convulsive agony. The Coroner's report makes uncomfortable reading: 'the body contained blisters which were filled with serum. This combined with inflammation of the mucous membrane meant she was alive while on fire.' It was a vicious and utterly inhuman crime which shocked the whole of the Channel Islands.

There was great pressure on the police to make an arrest. Mary de Jersey said she had seen a man she knew as Mr Simmer in the area soon after she had left Elizabeth Saujon's house. She knew

Quay Street, St Peter Port, where Tapner sometimes met his contacts in the town's criminal fraternity, *c.*1895. Reproduced by kind permission of the Priaulx Library, St Peter Port, Guernsey

that he had lodged at her friend's house for a short while. Mr Simmer had told her and Elizabeth that he was from St Martins. Police inquiries failed to locate any Mr Simmer from St Martins but they did establish that the name was an alias used by Tapner. John Charles Tapner was quickly arrested. He denied being in the area at all and he denied ever having met Elizabeth Saujon.

The circumstantial evidence was strong, however. It was proved that he had been in the given place at the given time, that he had lodged briefly with Elizabeth Saujon, and that he had begun to pay off his debts soon after the murder. After a trial which lasted twelve days he was found guilty of murder and robbery with arson and sentenced to death accordingly. Tapner volubly maintained his innocence and appealed to Queen Victoria for mercy. Victor Hugo, the renowned French writer and dissident, then in exile on Guernsey, supported Tapner in his appeal for clemency, on the grounds that all the evidence, though strong, was of a purely circumstantial nature.

The case had made news on the English mainland as well and Tapner's petition was turned down through the offices of Lord

Palmerston himself. As was the custom of the time, Tapner then gained a stay of execution through writing to the Court a full confession to the murder, but it was too little too late, although his execution was postponed from 27 January 1854 to 10 February that same year. It had been a cynical ploy, though he accepted that a reprieve was unlikely in the extreme. Far more mercy had already been shown towards him than he had been prepared to show his victim. He did not appear to be unduly perturbed that his time in this world was all but over, but in his last days Tapner was attended by two men of God, the Reverends Bouverie and Pearce, who spent time in his company and who prayed with him constantly as he prepared to meet his Maker.

Around six o'clock in the morning on 10 February, Tapner had his last meal, a breakfast of coffee and toast. Then he resumed praying with his chaplains until eight o'clock, the appointed hour for his execution. He left a brief letter for his wife, Mary, telling her that he felt better now that he had confessed his misdeeds and was going to pay the ultimate penalty for them. He did not write to her sister, Margaret, for whom he had risked so much. Just before eight o'clock he was led to the scaffold. Although his was not intended to be a public execution, the scaffold was clearly visible from St James' Church, Elizabeth College, Candie Road and Upland Road. The few private judicial witnesses were therefore joined by a multitude of public ones. The black hood was placed over Tapner's head, the noose around his neck, and the trapdoor opened. That should have been the end of Tapner's story, but it wasn't.

First, his hands had not been properly tied behind his back and he broke free as he struggled when the rope tightened. With his hands free he was able to hold on to the sides of the hatch through which he was meant to drop. The hatch was badly designed and too small to allow his freefall, so the executioner rushed down below and held on to Tapner's legs. Tapner screamed, then he twisted and convulsed as he was slowly strangled and this grotesque state of affairs continued for a full fifteen minutes before he was finally declared dead. The dreadful death of Elizabeth Saujon had been horribly avenged.

A large crowd had gathered by this time and, Guernsey being a very superstitious island, onlookers were convinced that if they could place the hands of Tapner's corpse on their faces they would be cured of diseases such as epilepsy. In addition souvenir hunters fought for pieces of the rope by which Tapner had died, until it was burned by the authorities. The whole episode was macabre beyond belief. Victor Hugo, the renowned French writer

Hauteville House, *c.*1920, where John Tapner's death mask is displayed. Author's collection

who had campaigned for Tapner's sentence to be commuted, bought the death mask made immediately after Tapner's execution for 3 francs. It is still possible to identify the swollen veins in his neck caused by his inhuman struggles. The mask is preserved in Hugo's former home, Hauteville House, to this day. The whole business had made a grisly and unedifying spectacle which put an end to capital punishment in Guernsey a full 111 years before the law of the land did so.

CHAPTER 3

The Sunny Bank Tragedy

1890

'His parents lived in harmony . . . he could only remember his father hitting his mother once . . .'

In the nineteenth century St Peter Port was an expanding town full of islanders and itinerant workers. Alcohol played a part in the social problems of the time, then as now, but the unusual aspect of this story is that the family were middle-class and could afford to live quite comfortably; the husband was in work and the wife stayed at home to raise their son and care for the house. On the surface all appeared to be well, but behind closed doors who knows what happens to turn people to drink and violence, which in this case resulted in a squalid, bloody and drunken murder.

Victoria Road leads off Trinity Square in the upper part of St Peter Port, rising gently as it winds its way north-west towards Grange Road. It is a quiet, sunlit street that houses a few small businesses, the States Archives, and a number of pleasant residences. The Sunny Bank of the title, which took its name from the sunny aspects of the street, no longer exists. Although there is still a house of a similar name in the street it is not the house in this story, being far too modern.

The committal for trial of Edward Bowden Hooper was reported by the local newspaper, *The Star*, on Tuesday 18 March 1890:

> *Edward Bowden Hooper, having on February 27 been brought before the [Royal] Court by . . . John Richard Harvey, one of the Constables . . . of St Peter Port, charged with having, either by himself, with or without accomplice or accomplices, without the fear of God, wilfully killed, slain and bruised Maria Pearce, wife of the said Hooper . . . having the night of 1st to the 2nd February 1890 . . . in a house occupied by him and his wife, situate in [Sunny Bank] Victoria Road, in . . . St Peter Port . . . at one or different*

Victoria Road from Pedvin Street, the quiet middle-class street where Edward Hooper killed his drunken wife, Maria. Reproduced by kind permission of the Priaulx Library, St Peter Port, Guernsey

times, assaulted, struck, beat and ill-used the said Pearce, and also dealt her violent blows to the head and body, whilst . . . [she] . . . was in a weak state of health from the immediate use of spiritous liquors [brandy], and the said Pearce dying in the morning of 2nd February 1890 in the aforesaid house, the death . . . being occasioned from the effects of blows and ill-usage received by her at the hands of . . . Hooper.

Both Hooper and his wife had been extremely drunk, having partaken of far more brandy than was prudent. Nothing had been seen of them from ten o'clock on the Saturday night until eleven o'clock the following morning, when Mrs Hooper was found dead, her body 'covered with wounds and abrasions and bruises'. It was reported that she was lying on the kitchen floor with her head under the table and her feet towards the fireplace. She had a wound on the back of her head and there was a broken chair with traces of blood and hair visible on it. The room was in complete disarray with broken glass everywhere. Blood was smeared all over the walls and furniture. Edward Hooper was just sitting in an armchair. He seemed dazed and said that his wife had originally been lying under the sofa but that he'd moved her. His brother William Hooper, said that Mrs Hooper was prone to fainting and often slept in the kitchen.

The first person to see Maria Hooper's inert body was the newsboy Frank Gill, who worked delivering newspapers for Mr Bichard's newsagents. However, he said that he had seen Mrs Hooper's body at three o'clock on the Saturday afternoon (1 February). He had not thought she was dead (although he supposed she could have been); just that she had fainted or passed out. It was probably not the first time that he had seen Mrs Hooper this way but he was expected to turn a blind eye, especially since the Hoopers were good customers. Frank Gill had given Mr Hooper his newspaper, received payment and had left the house. He said that he had not seen any broken glass.

The first cracks in the façade of respectability came with the evidence of Edward Hooper Jnr, the Hoopers' son. He had left home 'for reasons of comfort' and lived at the Albion Hotel on the seafront in St Peter Port. Ironically, the Albion holds the record for being the pub nearest to a church in the British Isles. He said that his parents 'lived in harmony' but his mother was unfortunately an alcoholic. He could only remember his father hitting his mother once. Six to seven weeks previously she had fallen down when she was drunk and cut her head. She had bled profusely and she'd had to wash the bloodstains off the sofa. She had also bruised and burned her arm falling against the stove. He was not present when the injuries occurred, nor was anyone else. Although it may have been born out of desperation at her alcoholism, it appeared that Edward Hooper beat his wife. It was also difficult to understand how Edward Jnr could say that his parents 'lived in harmony', given his evidence; and, if they did, why he had to leave home 'for reasons of comfort'? Why had he not helped his father to cope with his mother and the resultant domestic issues? He could have employed a maidservant to help his mother with the housework and provide company for her.

Edward Jnr's account of his mother's burn injury was confirmed by Louisa Collings. She had called with baker, James Waterman, at about a quarter to eight on the Saturday evening. She said they noticed that Mrs Hooper was on the hearthrug in her shift. She'd asked for clothing and the baker had covered her with a cloth. There was no broken glass, blood or disorder in the room. Mrs Hooper might have crawled under the sofa, where there were no bloodstains found, and then resisted her husband's efforts to move her. Mr Hooper might have dragged her and hit her as a result. She had never heard Maria Hooper complain about her husband.

Will Rowe, who worked for Mr Ozanne at his wine business, took six bottles of brandy to the house at about nine o'clock on Saturday night. He had also taken six bottles of brandy on the previous night, the Friday. Twelve bottles in twenty-four hours is a large amount of brandy. On the Saturday night, neighbour Annie Jackson, who had asked to fetch some water from the Hoopers' scullery, said she had heard Edward Hooper tell his wife 'get up you drunken thing', and then he had started swearing at her. The following morning she had returned to the house at about nine o'clock with Mr A Bowne, another neighbour who was a gardener, but all was very quiet. She believed that by that time Maria Hooper was dead.

Dr Clifford Crewe, who was called to the house around eleven o'clock on the Sunday morning, said that Hooper was still drunk and had bloodstains on his hands and clothes. Mrs Hooper lay in her shift on the blood-soaked carpet. She had sustained recent cuts and bruises to her body, face, arms and hands. There were bloodstains on the walls, the room was disordered and the chair was broken. Death had occurred between eight and nine o'clock that morning. The wounds could not have been self-inflicted and death was caused by shock. Mrs Brown, a charlady of Les Petites Fontaines, was called to lay out Mrs Hooper's body, washing and dressing her in preparation for her final journey, but it was a suspicious death and Dr Crewe had first called PC Lihou to the house. PC Lihou had also examined the body and the state of the room and he noted Edward Hooper's condition. After hearing their evidence HM Procureur (an official similar to the English Attorney General) said he did not think that the blow to the head would have killed a woman in ordinary health, but that it would be murder if she was in such a state that the blow had hastened her death.

The evidence continued. Alfred Pomeroy, who had happened to be passing by the house on Friday night, had heard Edward Hooper say to his wife, 'Go and lay down on your pillow or I'll kill you.' His statement was corroborated by Caleb Carré, who was walking with him. However, Hooper hotly refuted this and claimed that what he actually said was, 'Go and lay down on your pillow or *it* will kill you.' This sort of evidence could be taken as gossipy hearsay, but there was other evidence that life in the Hooper household was becoming fraught by the time of Maria Hooper's death. In a community like that on Victoria Road everyone knew everyone else and it was hard to keep secrets. Mrs

Roberts affirmed Louisa Collings' story of the burn wound and said that she'd also dressed another head wound for Mrs Hooper. Mrs Robilliard of Cordier Hill Steps on Victoria Road said that Mrs Hooper had a drink problem but that until recently Mr Hooper had been a sober, industrious, affectionate man. All the witnesses agreed that Mrs Hooper had been covered in bruises the previous October or November time. This may have been the result of a formerly loving husband finally snapping under the strain; or it may have been that the wife-beating normally accepted in Victorian society had become excessive in the case of Maria Hooper.

The Royal Court and the Jurats simply could not read the truth of the matter and indeed it was difficult to prove, under the circumstances, that Hooper had actually intended to kill his wife. Was it that he could stand no more of her drinking, of her embarrassing him in front of their friends and the tradespeople, of trying to clear up after her, and did he beat her to death in drunken frustration? Did he try and pull her from under the sofa to put her to bed, and when she resisted, did he simply lose his temper? Was he drunk himself and did he attack her? It was clear by this time that they were both drinking heavily. It was not questioned that he had hit her with varying degrees of force and frequency, because it was considered perfectly acceptable for a man to 'chastize' his wife, and many felt that Edward Hooper must have been sorely provoked by Maria Hooper's drinking. No one thought to ask why she had started drinking. The Royal Court could not decide on what had actually happened and in the end it was generally agreed that Hooper had 'accelerated' his wife's death by his actions and by his failure to seek medical help. His attack may not have been premeditated, but his not seeking appropriate medical help in time probably was deliberate. He had just sat there, in his chair, waiting, and watched her die. Accordingly he was sentenced to twenty years' penal servitude.

Chapter 4

A French Tragedy

1790

'The brothers were so shocked and shamed by this condemnation that both of them suffered strokes and died . . .'

The French Revolution spelled terror for many of the wealthy nobility, some of whom fled France with little more than their lives. As the fires of Paris raged and heads rolled at the Bastille, the upper classes of France were forced to flee for their lives, taking little except the clothes they stood up in and their memories of the menacing shadow of the guillotine. They left behind their lands, their homes, their friends, all that they held dear. Life is the most precious possession of all; but some did manage to take their money with them as well, only to find that it served them no better elsewhere than it had in France.

The Count de Daméque was one such nobleman, who fled his native city of Paris and took a house at Le Hurel above Le Vallon in St Martins on Guernsey. The Channel Islands are known to the French as the Anglo-Norman Isles and perhaps the Count felt that they would have something of his homeland about them. At least he could speak the language and on a clear day he could see country he loved lying low on the misty horizon. The Count wrote regularly to his friends in Paris and longed for the day when he could return. He kept himself to himself, which was hardly surprising in the circumstances, but it made him seem proud and aloof to local people. There being little else for him to do, he got into the habit of taking daily walks along the cliffs and country lanes. The south coast of Guernsey is steep and often treacherous, beautiful and, in many places, isolated, but the Count de Daméque always dressed well and expensively, as though he was going for a stroll along the Paris boulevards instead of a scramble across wild and rocky country. He strode through the country lanes and along the cliffs and could often be seen gazing wistfully out to sea, lost in his own thoughts. The Count de Daméque cut

The wooded countryside where the Count de Daméque took his walks and where he was eventually murdered. The defence tower was built during this time. The author

an imposing if unusual figure in St Martins and there were rumours that he regularly carried large sums of money with him.

One evening he failed to return to Le Hurel for dinner. It had been a pleasantly warm day and he had gone out for his walk as usual. It was thought that he had been heading in the direction of La Petite Porte, but no one was really sure. At first his staff were concerned but, after learning that he had been seen sailing away from Guernsey in the fishing boat he had hired for the season from Bec du Nez, they assumed that perhaps he had returned to France for some reason and that they would hear from him in due course. Such unquestioning acceptance might seem strange today but in the eighteenth century noble gentlemen felt that they did not have to explain themselves to anybody, least of all their servants.

However, one person was concerned. The Count de Daméque had a good friend in Paris named Dr Le Harrier. While in Guernsey he had written regularly to Dr Le Harrier, so the doctor was puzzled when the letters from the Count suddenly stopped. The two men had been good friends for a long time and such a silence on the part of the Count was most unusual. Dr Le Harrier wrote repeatedly to his friend's address at Le Hurel asking what had happened but his letters were never answered. However at that time the doctor was not free to travel to Guernsey to discover why his friend would not reply to him and sadly he accepted that the friendship must be at an end.

One day a few years later Dr Le Harrier was walking down a street in Paris when he saw a very unusual watch, bearing a coronet and arms on its case, hanging in a jeweller's window, and he recognized it at once as having belonged to his dear friend the Count de Daméque. He entered the shop and asked the jeweller how he had come by the watch. The jeweller said that some men from Guernsey had brought it in to him. They had tried unsuccessfully to sell the watch in England, Holland and Belgium and had finally come over to France to sell it. Dr Le Harrier bought the watch and took the address of the sellers. Returning home he quickly packed a small case and took the first available steamer to Guernsey.

There were two brothers, members of the Mauger family, living together in a cottage near Le Varclin in St Martins, not far from where the Count de Daméque had lived at Le Hurel. They drank, gambled, fought, and were generally regarded as the 'black sheep' of an otherwise respectable and hardworking family. It was their address which Dr Le Harrier had been given. On learning of their reputation when he arrived in Guernsey, Dr Le Harrier took the precaution of taking some police constables with him when he went to call on the brothers. When the party arrived at the cottage the brothers were drunk, but on seeing the watch in Dr Le Harrier's hands they broke down and confessed what they had done.

They had heard the rumours that the Count de Daméque was very rich and so one day they followed him on his walk along the cliffs. Above La Petite Porte he entered a narrow overgrown lane which led to Jerbourg Point. Here the brothers attacked and killed the Count. After robbing him of his watch, rings and such cash as he was carrying, they buried his body under a pile of stones lying on the edge of the cliffs. They then scuttled his boat and spread the rumour that he had been seen sailing for France. The brothers were arrested and handcuffed, and then, accompanied by the clergy, a doctor and practically all the inhabitants of St Martins, they led the way to the spot on the cliffs where they had murdered the Count.

When the doctor had certified that the bones were that of a complete male skeleton, the remains of the Count de Daméque were given a full Christian burial in the churchyard at St Martins. Afterwards one of the older parishioners, a man named Pierre Jehan, made a short sad speech at the graveside:

Formerly when burying a corpse one sent branches of trees and bouquets of flowers. Today there is nothing of that. Formerly one would have given a quarter of wheat rent to bear the name of Mauger. Today one would give four not to bear it.

The brothers were so shocked and shamed by this condemnation that both of them suffered strokes and died shortly afterwards in prison before they could be brought to trial.

The Count de Daméque was murdered very close to the spot where John Gordier (see Chapter 8, 'The Locket') had been murdered nearly a century before, and it was inevitable on such a deeply superstitious island that stories would begin to circulate of hauntings by the two victims in the narrow lanes around La Petite Porte, and ghostly cries were heard in the bay itself. These tales continued for a number of years. Finally, so the story goes, a man named Pierre Thoume, who lived at Les Blanches in St Martins, and who was a distant relative of the guilty Mauger brothers, volunteered to spend the night alone at the bay of La Petite Porte to try to 'lay the unquiet spirits'. He arrived at La Petite Porte at midnight, armed only with his Bible, and there he remained until the following morning. No one knows what happened. When he arrived home, pale and exhausted, Pierre Thoume refused to speak of what he had seen or of what he had done. He took his secret to the grave with him saying, 'I have given my word and I will not break it.' However, since the night he spent alone on the beach at La Petite Porte, there have been no more stories of hauntings by the two eighteenth-century murder victims or of mournful cries in the darkness of the lanes around Jerbourg.

CHAPTER 5

Watch the Wall My Darling

1828

'These midnight coffins were filled with contraband rather than corpses . . .'

All islands are good smuggling country. They are also often a 'back door' into certain countries, for the Revenue men do not have the manpower or resources for customs posts in every possible place where contraband might be brought ashore. For the authorities there is also the difficulty of policing coastlines which are usually remote, often treacherous, and offer a multitude of possible hiding places. For the smugglers these same coastlines offer multiple opportunities for concealing contraband goods such as caves or nicely hidden locations where smuggling caches can be built and perhaps reached by underground tunnels from the landing places. Underground tunnels were important in St Peter Port on Guernsey from Tudor times onwards. Smuggling has long been regarded as an acceptable way of supplementing income, especially in rural island communities, and Guernsey was ideally placed in many respects to build up a good smuggling empire.

King John is mostly known to the English as a 'bad king'. In the Channel Islands, however, King John is more kindly thought of, for his granting of generous privileges when the Islands decided to continue remaining loyal to the English Crown after the king had managed to lose Normandy back to the French. One of those privileges was the right to export to England without being liable for customs dues of any kind, which allowed the Islands to openly sell contraband goods to English smugglers.

Smuggling, or 'free trade' as it was known, reached its peak in the Guernsey Bailiwick during the late eighteenth century. In 1707 the British Government had tried in vain to establish a customs house in St Peter Port. Resistance to this move was led by Jurat William Le Marchant, who later became Bailiff of Guernsey. It was to be another sixty years before a customs house was finally established and even then there was fierce resistance. Outrunning and outwitting the 'preventatives', as customs men were generally known, became serious business. In February 1767 tougher measures had been taken to stop this practice but smuggling continued and in 1798 'free trading' lost the Crown over a million pounds (over £20 million in current-day value) in excise duties. In 1800 tougher measures were taken but such was the cunning of the Guernsey smugglers that it took years to successfully implement these measures. In 1805 the Lieutenant Governor offered a reward of 50 guineas for 'information leading to the apprehension of some evil-minded person who had bored several holes in the bottom of one of the boats belonging to His Majesty's Revenue'. Ironically, customs regulations today are stricter in the Channel Islands than anywhere within the European Union.

Alderney, with its proximity to the French coast, was ideal for smuggling wine, its remote and rocky shores affording a myriad of hiding places. The caves and cliffs of Sark, Brecqhou and Jethou also offered excellent places of concealment, and the south coast of Guernsey, particularly around Jerbourg, Le Petit Bôt, Saints Bay and Icart Point, is wild and lonely with several caves, so that legends of smuggling and pirates abound. The then remote west coast of Guernsey, especially around Perelle and Vazon, was also favoured because it was sparsely populated. It took two days to reach St Peter Port from Pleinmont, so customs officers stood little chance of catching smugglers 'in the act'. Guernsey was large enough and well placed between England and France to make it a favoured centre for the exchange of illicit goods. 'Trade' was done with Cornwall, the Isle of Wight, and probably the Isles of Scilly since those islands are on a similar latitude to the Channel Islands, and islanders made regular trips to France. Scillonians used six-oared gigs which could outrun the customs cutters; though cutters were often used by other smugglers because of their speed.

Tea was smuggled, especially French tea. In December 1828 twenty-one chests and four bags of tea were seized at Jerbourg. The previous year, before the introduction of French tea into Guernsey, 1,200 chests of tea were imported from England, whereas in 1828 only 260 such chests had been imported, which showed the scale of the trade in tea smuggling. The import tax on tea had risen to 96 per cent and such high import taxes made smuggling of tea inevitable. Tobacco (including shag and Virginian) was also smuggled. One dark windy night in 1870 the cutter *Mary* from Jersey was caught in Rocquaine Bay off Guernsey smuggling bales of both leaf and manufactured Kentucky tobacco. Acting on a tip-off the 'preventatives' quietly

Cliffs and caves near Icart Point on Guernsey's south coast. This type of coastline offered a haven to pirates and smugglers. The author

encircled the vessel in their boats under cover of darkness. Then two of their number created a diversion on the shore where a couple of smugglers had just landed their first load. The smugglers ran for their boat and rowed with all speed back out to the *Mary*, believing that they had given the officers the slip, only to find themselves surrounded and taken into custody. Nearly three tons of tobacco were retrieved and confiscated by customs officers, who had mounted a well-planned and organized operation and simply outwitted the smugglers. This episode shows the sheer scale of tobacco smuggling.

Brandy and wine were the chief smuggling commodities. So widespread was the smuggling of alcohol on the island that by 1805 there were 600 coopers in Guernsey making ten-gallon casks, which were easy to handle and ideal for the smuggling of brandy and other liquors. During the early nineteenth century one of Guernsey's most successful smugglers was a man named Jean Allaire, who lived at The Mount (now the Lieutenant

Governor's residence) on Queens Road. The house has a labyrinth of underground vaults ideal for secretly storing contraband. There are also said to be many houses in the areas of The Quay and Le Truchot in St Peter Port with similar vaults linked by a network of subterranean tunnels. Many islanders grew rich on the proceeds of smuggling and nowhere was the old adage 'Watch the wall my darling while the gentlemen go by' more appropriate than in the dark cobbled streets of Guernsey on moonless nights when all the smugglers had to guide them was the starlight dancing on the water.

The smugglers devised various ingenious ways of moving goods but the most popular seems to have been the 'funeral procession'. These midnight coffins were filled with contraband rather than corpses but most people, even 'preventatives', are loath to disturb a coffin. The smugglers, however, left little to chance. Guernsey is a deeply superstitious island so the wheels of the hearse were wrapped in sacking to muffle noise, as were the horses' hoofs, from which the shoes had been removed so that the animals' movements were silent; and the attendants 'had no heads', in order to give a thoroughly spooky and supernatural aspect to the whole procedure. Stories about phantom sows and piglets at Vazon, haunted lanes around the west and south coasts, ghostly goats or 'le bîche' (the beast) and the Devil in disguise abounded, some of them carefully put about to scare people away from certain areas at night. Often these tales were centred on the smugglers' favourite island haunts.

Would-be informers were dealt with in arbitrary and often brutal fashion, but as the nineteenth century wore on, the hated 'preventatives' became more successful and the smugglers' losses heavier. There were 700 packages in one haul seized by the customs men, including 400 of brandy, 140 of gin, 100 of rum and 60 bags of shag tobacco. One Customs and Excise official visited a local tobacco shop which had a very large store of tobacco. When he questioned the owner the man was apologetic in his reply. 'Yes, I know, but my boys they smokes a lot!' There is a tale that the last of the Guernsey smugglers were caught around 1880 when several barrels of brandy were found buried in a field near a chapel on the Paysans road close to L'Erée Hotel.

Despite everything, there was something of the *Boys' Own* daring cavalier about smugglers simply trying to provide a decent drink and a good smoke for their fellow men and many simply turned a good-natured blind eye. There was after all something infinitely satisfying about 'putting one over' on the Chancellor of the Exchequer. There still is, and most people will try to bring back that extra bottle of wine from some foreign land, but today smuggling has taken a sinister downturn. There are fortunes to be made from smuggling drugs and trading in other people's misery and there is no romance or daring about that. The days of silent shadowy figures leading eerie midnight hearses and the tales of phantom pigs and ghostly goats are gone, perhaps forever.

Chapter 6

A Pointless Death

1829

'. . . placing his knee upon his body . . . produced an extraversion of blood on the brain . . . causing instant death.'

The nineteenth century was a period of great expansion in Guernsey with shipbuilding, quarrying and construction providing work for both local people and itinerant workers from France, England, Belgium and other western European countries. Away from family and friends, there was little diversion for these workers and drinking, often heavily, was a popular pastime. There were a number of public houses in St Peter Port well frequented by both the foreign workers and visiting sailors. The ale flowed, sometimes tempers flared, and occasionally violence exploded.

Berthelot Street is a steep narrow little street which leads off the High Street in St Peter Port. In former times the sea used to come up as far as the High Street, and Berthelot Street, then the main road to the Grange, was a busier more important place than the backwater it has become today. There was one large old house on the street, which had once belonged to a wealthy merchant and his wife, from which a tunnel ran underground to the Town Church. The street had a bad reputation, though, and throughout the nineteenth century it was reputed to be haunted by a number of ghosts, especially near the top end, where there was a junction with Lefebvre Street. Guernsey folk therefore gave the area a wide berth after darkness had fallen, and it was generally pretty much deserted at night.

On a warm day in August 1829 two Frenchmen, Louis Homnés and Guillaume-Marie André, from René in Brittany, were looking forward to an evening's hard drinking after a heavy day spent hewing stone. Both of them had a thirst. The temperature on a Guernsey summer's day can reach 24 or 25 degrees and when there is no wind it can feel extremely hot. Louis and Guillaume-Marie were strong young men and worked hard. By the time they downed tools for the day, their throats were parched. At the first decent beerhouse they came to on their way home they stopped and quenched their thirst, before deciding how and where to spend the rest of their evening. As usual they decided on a tour of the pubs, before ending the night's entertainment back in Berthelot Street. They wound their way up the narrow cobbled Le Pollet, chattering in rapid excited French and breaking into occasional bursts of loud song.

The moon was high in the sky when they finally staggered into Berthelot Street in a very drunken state. Both men were tired now and becoming a trifle tetchy. What started as some minor point of contention escalated rapidly, as can happen when the protagonists are both drunk. Voices were raised and fingers wagged in faces. There was some pushing and jostling and a scuffle broke out between the two men. Neither man was steady and a mis-timed punch caught Louis Homnés unawares. He fell to the ground and lay still. This appeared to incense André, who then lost his temper completely. He kicked and pummelled Homnés mercilessly as he lay on the ground and within a very short time Louis Homnés was dead.

Afterwards André claimed that Homnés was very drunk and that during their quarrel Homnés had seized him by the neckerchief and would have strangled him if they had not been separated. André had then lost his temper, a drunken scuffle had ensued and Homnés fell backwards, hitting his head. There had been hardly any witnesses, owing to the reputation of the street, but André's version did not quite tally with medical evidence. It is doubtful, though, whether André could remember properly anything that had happened and it is probable that he had not actually intended to kill Homnés.

Guillaume-Marie André was brought before the Royal Court and committed for trial for 'having feloniously killed the said Homnés [on Monday 10 August] by giving him several blows, and by placing his knee upon his body when on the ground which produced an extraversion of blood on the brain, thereby causing instant death'. Although Homnés had hit his head on the pavement and had been knocked out, it was the kicking he had received from André which had killed him. André, however, claimed that he had acted in self-defence and had not meant to kill Homnés.

The trial was held at the Royal Court on Saturday 22 August. Advocate Jeremie defended André, while the Solicitor General, and Advocate de Sausmarez, delegate Attorney General, acted for the prosecution. The magistrates could not decide if André should be imprisoned or not. After all, a man had died, but it had been an accident (albeit with contributory negligence) rather than a premeditated act of violence. Five magistrates believed André should be imprisoned for up to six weeks and three believed he should be acquitted. Finally, the Bailiff, mindful that though it had been a drunken squabble, Louis Homnés' death was accidental, decided to acquit André, and so Guillaume-Marie André walked from the Royal Court a free man.

CHAPTER 7

Call of the Werewolf

1632

'She dragged herself to her feet bruised, bleeding, crying and in pain . . .'

Werewolves are something usually vaguely associated in the public mind with Transylvania and B-class horror movies. After all, in real life people don't, in fact can't, just metamorphose into hungry demented wolverine creatures simply because there is a full moon. There is a long tradition of werewolves (the name originates from the Anglo-Saxon *wer*, meaning man) which stretches back into prehistory, and the story of Little Red Riding Hood, published by the Brothers Grimm in 1812, was a tale which may well have had its origins in werewolfery. 'Man wolves' could also be the result of genetic hair-growing disorders or a mental disorder known as lycanthropy which causes the sufferer to fantasize about being a wolf. One website (www.arkanefx.com) gives the physical characteristics of people with werewolf tendencies as having eyebrows which knit together in the middle of the forehead, long or curved fingernails, small flat or pointed ears low on the head, and the second and third fingers on each hand of equal length.

In France and the Channel Islands there is a particularly strong werewolf tradition known as 'vouarouverie', but it has little to do with the popular conception. There is also an exceptionally strong tradition of the Devil, who can appear in many guises, the werewolf being a popular one, but on Sark and Guernsey especially it was often more to do with a licence for young men to misbehave than with any supernatural or devilish origins. The 'misbehaviour' was actually pretty serious and included theft, assault, gross overeating, drunkenness and rape. There was a local belief that often the practice of werewolfery, the 'damnable art', evolved through social misfits and petty criminals banding together into groups of 'de damnatis'.

There are a number of commemorative werewolf names, such

The Devil with his witches at 'Le Trepied'. He is in the guise of a werewolf. Illustration: Hannah Niblet

as Le Courtil Variouf, La Rocque Variouf, Les Varioufs (in St Martins), and the district of Les Varioufs near Petit Bôt. The name Le Courtil (field) Variouf is frequently found in Guernsey near the sites of dolmens and menhirs, so perhaps once there was some sort of ancient ritual connection. There were bands of werewolves all over Northern Europe – in Normandy, Germany, France, Prussia, Livonia, Lithuania, the Channel Islands – members of an 'evil confraternity' who were especially active during the Christmas season, when they 'indulged in gluttonous feastings and bacchanal orgies of drunkenness and debauchery'. In Guernsey throughout the sixteenth and seventeenth centuries werewolves attacked people, ravaged livestock, drank to excess (often whole casks of beer at a time) and raped any women unlucky enough to cross their paths.

The werewolves disguised themselves in animal skins 'putting on such monstrous shapes that it were hard to say whether they were more worthy of laughter or of tears . . . they disguise themselves so skilfully, some with the head, some with the skins of some beast or other'. Animal skulls and skins were carefully hoarded and hidden on the island for this purpose, and in Sark as late as the nineteenth century horse skulls were still kept in many households.

In 1600 a young Breton girl, Judith Le Blocq, who was on trial by the Royal Court in Guernsey for infanticide, said that she had been subjected to an attack by a group of werewolves. In modern terminology this would have involved a 'gang rape' and if her

Le Petit Bôt on Guernsey's south coast. There are holy wells in the woods and the high ground about is Le Variouf district (Land of the Werewolf). The author

child was the result of that, then it may have been the reason why she killed her baby. Five men were tried in 1630 on a charge that they were werewolves and that they 'had been disguised by night under a most hideous and shocking form', but their crimes are not listed.

In 1631 and 1632 there were trials on Guernsey for cases of werewolfery, both occurring in St Martins, and in the latter case five men, who included Collas Mauger, James le Retillay, Abraham Sandre, Thomas Blanche and Daniel Rabay, were accused of 'going about in werewolfery'. The five had returned from Town (St Peter Port) where they had been drinking heavily. They were drunk, swearing, and out for mischief. Arriving home late at night in St Martins, their thirst renewed from the uphill trudge, they decided that 'it was good weather to go about in werewolfery'. Gathering themselves together under a thorn bush they embraced and uttered oaths, as was the custom before beginning their 'werewolfery activities'. The men were then charged with 'having by night and at an improper hour, beat with stones on the door of widow or spinster Thomasse Guignon's until she

Les Varioufs in St Martins, the name commemorating the 'bands of were-wolfery' who went on the rampage here. The author

was made to rise from her bed . . . and to commit other insolences and a deed most heinous'.

The distressed woman told the Royal Court that she had gone to bed soon after nightfall that evening and that she had been awakened in the middle of the night by stones being thrown at her door. At first she had ignored the knocking and shouted at the perpetrators to go away before falling asleep again. The 'were-wolves' were not to be put off so easily however. They woke her up again with their incessant calls and yells and throwing stones at her windows. Sleepily she answered what she thought might be a neighbour's knocks at the door and realized her mistake too late as she lifted the catch. The men burst into her cottage and grabbed hold of her, dragging her back into the living room. At first they just made lewd comments, which she did her best to ignore, and ordered her to fetch some ale. Hoping desperately that they would leave her alone if she complied with their request she fetched a jug of ale. However, the alcohol simply served to inflame their passions. Four of the men spread-eagled her roughly on the floor, each man holding an arm or a leg. She began to scream and a calloused hand was clamped roughly over her mouth so that she could hardly breathe. The fifth man had then brutally raped her. When he had finished he got up and spat on her. Each of the remaining four men then took it in turns to rape her. Afterwards they had kicked her aside like a bundle of dirty rags as they left the house. She had dragged herself to her feet bruised, bleeding, crying and in pain, too shocked to do anything except crawl into her bed. Next morning she had gone to her neighbour's farmhouse and collapsed.

However for the 'band going about in werewolfery' the night was still young. They next broke into the cellar of one of the larger houses in the district and on discovering a number of barrels full of beer set up a cheer. Having partaken of liquid refreshment, they then raided the pantry. If the householder heard them he or she sensibly put their head under the sheets and kept very quiet. By now it was not far off dawn and a young serving girl was walking to her work. There were a number of itinerant young female servants on Guernsey who travelled from house to house offering their services. These girls were very vulnerable to random attacks and were regarded as fair prey by the bands of werewolves who prowled about the countryside. This particular girl, whose name has been lost to history, became suddenly aware of the five men blocking her path. She knew what it meant and uttering a single loud scream she turned and ran. Sadly, they were too fast and too strong for her. She too was brutally gang-raped in the same manner as Thomasse Guignon and then tossed aside. Unfortunately for her, this girl was also young enough to become pregnant as a result of the rapes. It is not recorded whether this happened or not, but if it did result in her giving birth to a child conceived in such a manner she may well have ended up like the unhappy Judith Le Blocq who had killed her baby.

The band of werewolves was now beginning to run out of steam. Turning for home, they savaged and killed a couple of hapless sheep grazing in a field nearby almost as an afterthought before giving their final yowls of the night. It was a horrendous catalogue of behaviour, crime and violence which sadly had become commonplace on the island. During the sixteenth century one of Guernsey's problems seemed to be that it was 'full of yowthe', and as in more recent times, that 'yowthe' was bored and looking for trouble 'by nocturnal and tenebrous companies which run and gad by night from house to house around this island, some masked, others with cudgels and disguised, committing an infinity of insolences and debaucheries, to the dishonour of God, contempt of court and public dread'.

Punishment in these cases was public suspension from the Eucharist, which meant public shame and excommunication from the Church, so that their immortal souls were imperilled. Thomasse Guignon had the courage to bring her tormentors to trial. They were local men and of course she had recognized all of them. Collas Mauger, James le Retillay, Abraham Sandre, Thomas Blanche and Daniel Rabay were duly tried and found guilty by the Guernsey Royal Court and publicly deprived of the Eucharist and the blessing of the Church. In Jersey the Royal Court had ruled that 'those who shall be convicted . . . of having run by night disguised and with cudgels from which issue an infinity of debauchery and scandals and also those who dance in public shall publicly be deprived of the Eucharist'. However, it did not generally seem to act as much of a deterrent and 'de damnatis' continued their unholy practices until at least the eighteenth century, with commemoration of the tradition lasting into the early twentieth century, when Hollywood took over the preservation of this particular folk memory.

Chapter 8

The Locket

1700

'None but those who have experienced the furious impulse of ungovernable love will pardon the crime which I have committed . . .'

There are a number of families on Guernsey able to trace their origins to early medieval times. Of course, everyone alive today must have had medieval (and even earlier) ancestors, but as the hero of one historical novel put it, 'The difference between us and our coachman out there is that we know the names of our ancestors and he doesn't'. The Mauger family are a very old family on Guernsey, said to be able to trace their roots back to the time of William the Conqueror. However, this sad story of love, jealousy, murder and betrayal concerning a young and beautiful descendant of William's uncle, Mauger, Archbishop of Rouen, happened nearly seven hundred years after the Conqueror's ships first sailed into Guernsey.

Rachel would appear to be a family name of the Maugers handed down generation after generation. Rachel Mauger, the heroine of this story, lived at Le Varclin in St Martin round about the year 1700. She was a renowned beauty of her time and, as her parents were wealthy, she was eagerly sought after by a number of young men. A local man named Gaillard, who worked as a clerk for her father, fell hopelessly in love with Rachel. Over the years he worked hard and became a very prosperous merchant in St Peter Port and he desperately wanted to marry her, but she refused because she had given her heart to someone else, a Frenchman born on Jersey named John Andrew Gordier. Rachel Mauger was not only a romantic but she was a woman true to her word and her heart.

One morning in the early summer of 1701 or 1702 she received word that her adored fiancé was sailing over to Guernsey from Jersey that day to see her. Rachel was deeply in love and she could hardly wait to see him. She read and re-read his note until she knew it by heart. He had asked her if she would meet him at La Petite Porte on Guernsey's southern coast because it was the nearest landing place to her house. They could have a few precious minutes alone together before joining the rest of the family. Gaillard also chose that same morning to come and call upon Rachel, though she never saw him because he had been turned away from the house as everyone was preparing for John Gordier's visit. Reluctantly and resentfully, Gaillard took his leave. In great excitement Rachel got herself ready for John's arrival and then, wearing her best dress and bonnet, left the house to walk down to La Petite Porte.

Gaillard happened to be sitting a little way above the bay of La Petite Porte, brooding and sulking over the situation with Rachel, when he saw John Gordier's boat coming in to land. Consumed with jealousy, he watched Gordier tie up his boat and start to climb the winding path up the cliff to the windmill at Moulin Huet. Rachel had not yet arrived and suddenly Gaillard saw that he had been presented with an unexpected opportunity to get rid of his hated rival once and for all. Quickly taking out the knife that he always carried for protection, he hid behind a large

La Petite Porte where John Gordier landed shortly before he met his death. The author

boulder. He watched John Gordier stride up the path towards him, happy in anticipation of seeing his Rachel again. Gaillard could hardly bear to look at him and as Gordier passed the boulder where Gaillard had hidden himself, Gaillard ran up behind him and stabbed him twice in the back. John Gordier collapsed instantly without a sound. Gaillard, looking furtively about him to see that no one was around, dragged Gordier's body to a nearby small cave just below the path, where he quickly concealed it. Before leaving the cave, Gaillard searched Gordier's body and found a small locket in one of his pockets which he was bringing as a present for Rachel. Slipping the locket into his own pocket, Gaillard made his escape.

Rachel arrived at La Petite Porte and, seeing John Gordier's boat tied up there, ran expectantly towards it. He was not there. She looked around, puzzled. Somehow she must have missed him. Disappointed, she began the long climb back up the cliffs towards her home. The sun was now high in the sky and the day was hot, and she wished desperately that she had his arm to lean upon. When Rachel finally arrived back at Le Varclin she was astonished to discover that he was not there. Then she was worried. What on earth had become of him? Concerned as well, her father sent out a search party but there was no trace of John Gordier. He seemed to have vanished completely.

Rachel was distraught at Gordier's disappearance. She couldn't understand it. The searchers continued to hunt for him and finally his body was discovered in the cave. When it became obvious that he had been murdered, Rachel was completely grief-stricken and heartbroken. John Gordier had been her soul-mate, the love of her life. She felt that she had no future now that he was dead, but her family determined that she should marry Gaillard instead. Rachel wasn't interested but they put a lot of pressure on her to allow Gaillard to court her. He was, after all, a rich man, and therefore a good catch. Gaillard was absolutely overjoyed at this turn of events and called on her regularly, pretending not to notice her lack of enthusiasm. It was natural that she should grieve, he told himself. It would pass. One day, to try to cheer her, he gave her the locket as a present. Rachel did not want to wear his gift but her parents insisted that she must and very reluctantly she wore it on her watch-chain.

Shortly afterwards Mrs Gordier arrived from Jersey to visit her dead son's intended wife and pay her condolences. Rachel was by now in a terrible state. She was consumed by her grief, unable to eat or sleep properly, and in a very weak condition. When she saw her beloved John's mother she fainted. Mrs Gordier was shocked and tried to comfort her, but every time that John's name was mentioned Rachel fainted again. Then Mrs Gordier saw the locket that Rachel was wearing. She knew that her son had ordered it to be made specially for Rachel before he had left Jersey for the last time. Appalled, she told Rachel, and asked sternly how Rachel had come by the locket. Rachel stared at her uncomprehendingly before realizing in horror that it must have been Gaillard who had murdered her darling John. She put her hand to her mouth and, clutching at the locket as though she would pull it from her, she murmured faintly 'clerc'. Then she collapsed and died.

Mrs Gordier mistook Rachel's grief for guilt. She called for Rachel's parents and accused the dead girl of being an accomplice to her son's murder. There was a furious quarrel and Rachel's father tried to order Mrs Gordier from the house, but Mrs Gordier would not be moved. She insisted that she was telling the truth and proved to them that the locket was the same one her son had ordered by touching a hidden spring which opened to reveal her son's portrait concealed in the locket. Through her tears, Rachel's mother asked if her daughter had said anything before she died. Mrs Gordier snapped that Rachel had muttered something about a clerk but how was she supposed to judge if that had meant anything. Horrified, Rachel's parents looked at each other. Knowing that Gaillard had given Rachel the locket, they sent for him at once. Asked to explain how he came to have the locket in his possession, Gaillard said smoothly that he had purchased it from a Jewish pedlar named Levi who visited Guernsey from time to time. He thought it a pretty thing and that Rachel would like it. The pedlar was immediately tracked down and taken into custody to stand trial, although he protested his innocence vociferously.

However, on the morning on which Levi the pedlar was due to be brought before the Royal Court, there was a further sensation. Gaillard was found stabbed to death. It appeared that finally his guilt, remorse, shame, and the loss of his beloved Rachel had become too much for him to bear and he had killed himself, leaving behind a letter confessing his crime. By way of justification for the murder of John Gordier he wrote:

'None but those who have experienced the furious impulse of ungovernable love will pardon the crime which I have committed, in order to obtain the incomparable object by whom my passions were inflamed.'

It was a poor excuse, although the Court had no alternative but to accept it. Three people had died because of Gaillard's 'inflamed passions'. It is not recorded if either Rachel's parents or Mrs Gordier pardoned Gaillard. But if Gaillard had really loved Rachel as much as he claimed, her happiness would have been of the utmost importance to him. The truth was that he did not love her enough to let her go.

CHAPTER 9

The Pirates of Jethou and Brecqhou

1717

'. . . islands . . . of pirates, thieves, brigands, murderers and assassins . . . [where] they kill boys for beef . . .'

In modern times piracy has been regarded as a swashbuckling and romantic affair and has most recently been celebrated in the award-winning and very funny film *Pirates of the Caribbean*. But real pirates were nothing like Johnny Depp's sympathetic and somewhat camp portrayal. Their methods were often brutal and violent. As on

Jethou, 1908, where the remains of the gibbet from which pirates were hanged can still be seen. Reproduced by kind permission of the Priaulx Library, St Peter Port, Guernsey

other offshore islands of Britain in the sixteenth to eighteenth centuries, pirates made a terrible nuisance of themselves in the Channel Islands which, with their rocky cliffs, hidden caves and coves, especially those of Sark, Brecqhou and Jethou, and Guernsey's south coast, were ideal for pirating activities.

Jean Allaire, one of Guernsey's most successful smugglers, was a former tenant of Jethou. In 1717 piracy and smuggling was one of the main subsistence industries on Jethou, and the remains of a gibbet, where some of the unluckier pirates and smugglers paid the supreme penalty, can still be seen deep in Keitholm Wood. Brecqhou, separated from Sark by just 73 metres of water, has its Cave aux Pirates on the south-eastern side of the island. The Cave is accessible only by boat and, according to J L V Cachemaille, vicar of Sark in the mid-nineteenth century, 'a narrow cleft at the inner end' led to a 'hidden maze of caves which honeycombe the island'. Cachemaille wrote of 'an immense heap of cinders' on the beach of this cleft. Legend says that the cave system was inhabited by rats whose first colony 'deserted a sinking ship' near the island in 1665. It seems that both rats and passengers were trying to escape the Black Death which was ravaging London.

There is an amusing story that in the late sixteenth century English pirates stole three cows from Guernsey and headed for

The iron ring which held gibbets in Keitholm Wood on Jethou where pirates were executed in the sixteenth and seventeenth centuries. The author

Brecqhou, then popular for rabbiting. On the way they intercepted a Sark boat returning from Guernsey, stole a silver pin from Janette du Val (one of the passengers) and a barrel of beer, and took crew member John Hotton hostage, because he was said to be a good pilot, and probably also as a guarantee of safe passage. However, Hotton managed to escape when his captors tried to pillage an Alderney boat, but were driven off when another boat was sighted close by. The pirates and their haul of live cows were eventually captured by Bretons. Sark itself, with its impossible cliffs, proved a haven for pirates until 1549 when a French invasion force put an abrupt end to their activities. During the 1530s Rabelais wrote 'Let us never descend to the lands of thieves and robbers . . . in the islands of Sark and Herm . . . isles of pirates, thieves, brigands, murderers and assassins . . . [where] they kill boys for beef'. Sark still has an impenetrably majestic air but, standing on beautiful peaceful Herm today with its golden sands and the seabirds wheeling nonchalantly over the southern cliffs, it is hard to credit the island with his description.

The western coast of Herm today near Puffin Bay, where pirates are said to have 'eaten boys for breakfast'. The author

Chapter 10

Daylight Robbery

1689–1856

'. . . we have received divers complaints of great irregularities and unjustifiable violences committed by our privateers . . .'

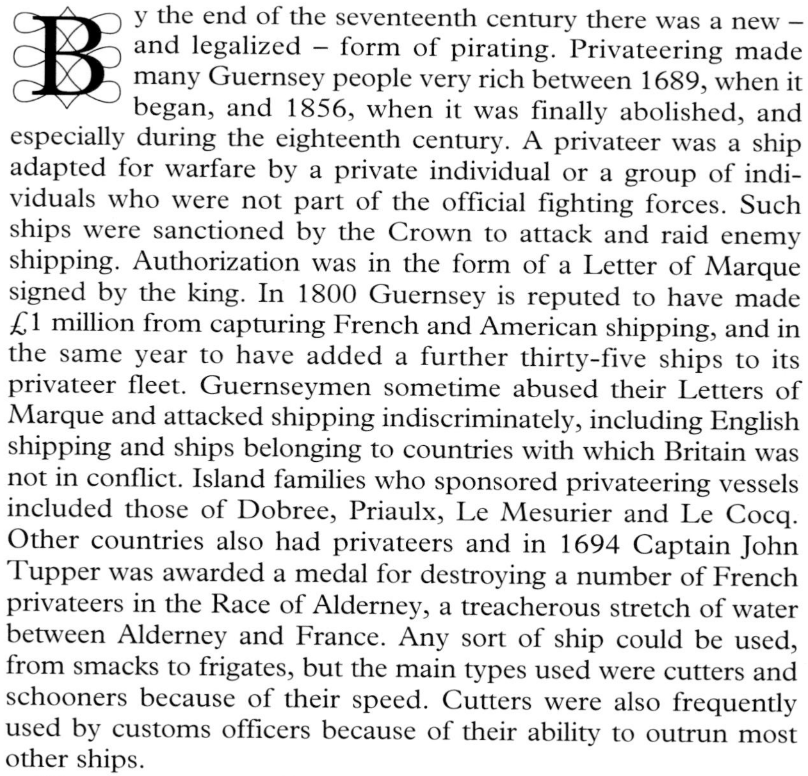

By the end of the seventeenth century there was a new – and legalized – form of pirating. Privateering made many Guernsey people very rich between 1689, when it began, and 1856, when it was finally abolished, and especially during the eighteenth century. A privateer was a ship adapted for warfare by a private individual or a group of individuals who were not part of the official fighting forces. Such ships were sanctioned by the Crown to attack and raid enemy shipping. Authorization was in the form of a Letter of Marque signed by the king. In 1800 Guernsey is reputed to have made £1 million from capturing French and American shipping, and in the same year to have added a further thirty-five ships to its privateer fleet. Guernseymen sometime abused their Letters of Marque and attacked shipping indiscriminately, including English shipping and ships belonging to countries with which Britain was not in conflict. Island families who sponsored privateering vessels included those of Dobree, Priaulx, Le Mesurier and Le Cocq. Other countries also had privateers and in 1694 Captain John Tupper was awarded a medal for destroying a number of French privateers in the Race of Alderney, a treacherous stretch of water between Alderney and France. Any sort of ship could be used, from smacks to frigates, but the main types used were cutters and schooners because of their speed. Cutters were also frequently used by customs officers because of their ability to outrun most other ships.

There were proper 'Articles of Agreement' between the owner or owners of the ship and the officers and crew. Fourteen clauses laid down terms and conditions and how many shares in goods and cargoes seized should be received by each crew member. This could be dependent on rank and also on the contribution made by each crew member to a particular 'cruise', as their armed expeditions were known. For example, on an expedition undertaken by the Guernsey privateer *Admiral Sausmarez* in 1805, the sailing master and the doctor each received fifty shares, and the gunner and the carpenter twenty shares each, while at the lower end of the scale two ordinary seamen received ten shares each but a third colleague only received six shares. This may not have amounted to much in some cases, as a fifth of the total went to the king and two-thirds of the remainder to the owners, which left just four-fifteenths to be divided between the crew.

On the other hand, the rewards could be high. A St Domingo ship captured in March 1779 and taken to Guernsey was valued at between £30,000 and £50,000 (between £1.5 and £2.5 million at present-day values); two French East Indiamen, captured in the August of that year by the privateer *Guernsey* were worth £120,000 each (around £6 million at current values); and the *Signora Mercantolia* (sailing from Cadiz to Nantes) was valued at £40,000 (£2 million today). There were valuable, if not exactly military, cargoes to be captured, which included silk, cotton, hides, cocoa, wine, brandy, rum, sugar, coffee, oil, spices, nutmegs, tortoiseshells and Dutch knives. The strangest must surely have been that of 116 elephant teeth. Ships were also frequently ransomed by the privateers, though this was strictly against orders.

Clause Seven of the Articles of Agreement stated that there should be no plundering, which seems absurd, given that this was the whole aim of the attacks made by these privateers, but it doubtless meant that once the captured cargo was on board, individual crew members should not help themselves but were to wait until the official share-out, thereby confirming the old saying about 'honour among thieves'. The intention of licensing privateers was to give French, Spanish and American shipping a hard time and to recoup some of the losses incurred during the fighting that occurred between these nations and Britain during the eighteenth century, and also to act as spies and gather information which might be useful to the British Government. Of course it didn't work that way. Some privateers became over-zealous or plain greedy, attacking ships of both friendly and neutral nations indiscriminately.

First to complain were the Dutch. It was not the first time the Dutch had suffered in this way. During the English Civil War of the preceding century, Dutch shipping had been regularly attacked by the inhabitants of the Isles of Scilly (which lie 43 kilometres south-west of Cornwall on a similar latitude to Guernsey), in order to help the Royalist cause. This had annoyed the Dutch, so much so that in 1651 they declared war on the Scillies and an alarmed Cromwell was forced to send one of his best admirals to the Scillies to defend the islands and sort out the situation. However, just thirty-seven years later, a Dutchman, King William of Orange, sat on the throne of England and Scotland as King William III and ruled the country jointly with his wife, Mary II. The Dutch had been confident that this uniting of the two countries would bring an end to the offensive on their shipping by the British, but William died in 1702 without issue and a few decades later Dutch ships were being plundered once more, this time by the privateers from the Channel Islands who were supposed to owe their allegiance to the English Crown.

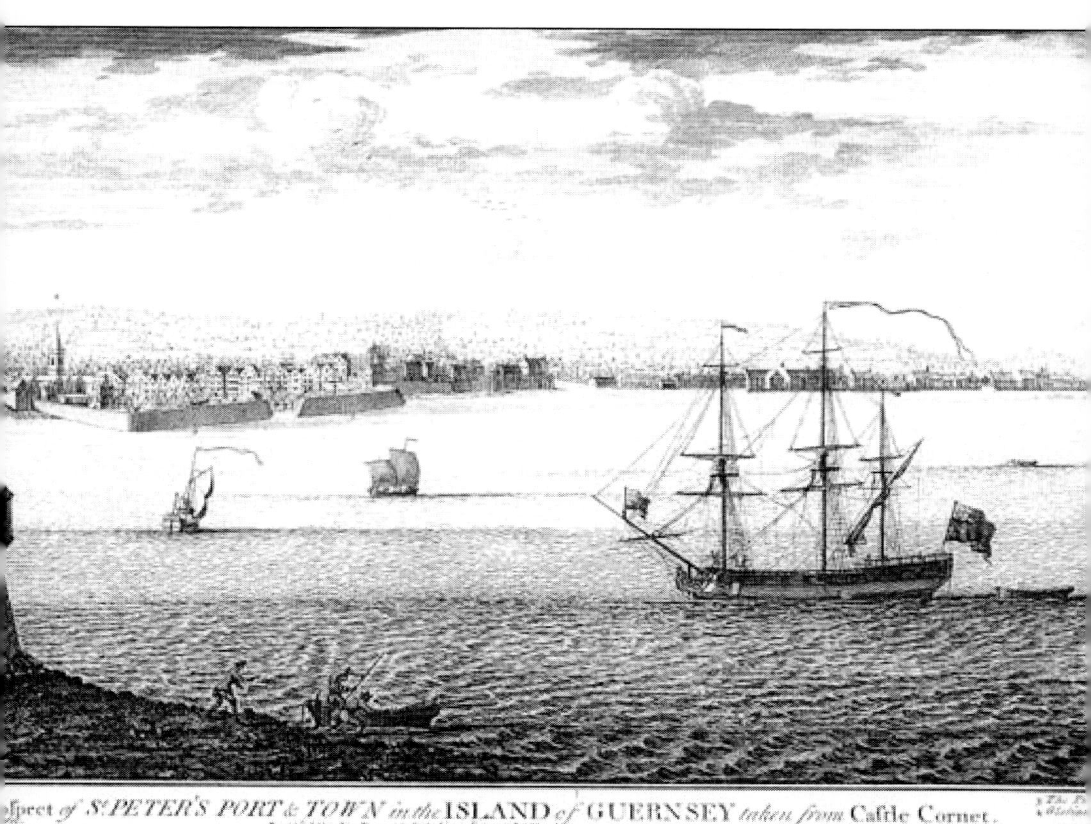

Eighteenth-century prospect of St Peter Port, showing the town during the heyday of the privateers. Reproduced by kind permission of the Priaulx Library, St Peter Port, Guernsey

The Dutch grievances were followed by complaints from Denmark, Tuscany, Egypt, Turkey and the Ottoman Empire. A Danish brig, with a cargo of brandy, was taken in Gibraltar as well, and a Portuguese brig was also captured. Finally the Guernsey privateers began attacking English ships. In 1777 a kind of 'bail system' was introduced whereby owners of privateers had to pay a deposit of £1,500 (for a ship with a crew of less than 150) or £3,000 (for ships which had larger crews), which would be forfeited if their ship attacked the shipping of any country which was not at war with England and which was not an enemy. This measure clearly did not work, however, for the attacks continued and the commanders of privateers encouraged the defection of English sailors to privateering by bribing them with the offer of large bounties. The following year, in November 1778, a warning was issued that misuse of a Letter of Marque in this way would incur 'our [the king's] highest displeasure and such penalty as by law may be inflicted'.

A month later a clearly exasperated George III, who had already given privateers a warning about attacking ships of the Ottoman Empire and subjects of the 'Grand Signor', issued a much more serious warning:

> *Whereas Commanders of merchant ships that have obtained Letters of Marque are authorized to take only ships, etc., belonging to the French King or his vassals and subjects and in no wise to attempt anything against the ships, etc., or any other prince or state in amity with us. Notwithstanding which we have received divers complaints of great irregularities and unjustifiable violences committed by our privateers by seizing the ships etc., of the subjects of such princes and states.*
>
> *For the avoiding for the future all such irregularities and to remove every possible cause for complaint we do hereby strictly charge and enjoin the commanders and crews of all vessels having Letters of Marque that they do not under any pretence seize or detain any such ship etc. (such goods not being warlike or naval stores) unless they shall have probable ground to suspect that the evidence offered as to the property of such ship and goods is fraudulent and untrue . . . and it having been particularly represented unto us, that notwithstanding the orders which we have given to prevent the capture of any Dutch ships laden with innocent cargoes, vessels of that description continue to be taken . . . we do hereby strictly charge the commanders of such privateers that they do not on any account seize or detain any ship belonging either to the States-General [Holland] of the United Provinces or their subjects.*

George III's difficulty, however, was that the privateers were out of control. Between 1793 and 1801, 235 Letters of Marque were issued, followed by a further 602 between 1803 and 1814. This meant that Guernsey men had been given official royal permission on 837 occasions to attack shipping that supposedly belonged to the enemies of the British Crown and their allies, or which were carrying a military cargo. It was a recipe open to widely differing interpretations. The king had his own problems as well, in that he had developed a serious medical condition which appeared to rob him of his sanity, and for much of the latter part of his reign his eldest son, who was to become George IV, acted as Regent. Doctors now believe that George III suffered from an aversion to sunlight. The doctors of the time, however, not realizing this, recommended that the king take as much fresh air and sunshine as possible, which simply made his condition worse. Meanwhile this left the privateers to do pretty much as they pleased. In one year alone they took 608 ships. Families grew rich. The Spanish treasure galleon *Cobadonga* was captured in 1743 by the privateer *Centurion*, whose First Lieutenant was Philip Sausmarez. It has been estimated that she was carrying around £800,000 sterling (worth over £60 million at present-day values).

The proceeds of this venture enabled an old Guernsey family to regain their ancestral home. In 1557 Sausmarez Manor had passed to the Andros family through the marriage of Judith de Sausmarez to John Andros. Their son built the Tudor house in 1585 at right angles to the original medieval manor. (Part of this house is still used by a coppersmith, who makes reproduction Guernsey milk churns, in the form of a lidded jug, the design of which is the same as those used in Norman times.) The present Queen Anne house was built between 1714 and 1718 according to the will of Sir Edmund Andros, who in 1674 had been both Bailiff of Guernsey and Governor of New York. To him goes the credit of renaming the city New York. (It had previously been known as New Amsterdam.) It had long been the ambition of the Sausmarez family to own Sausmarez Manor once more, and this was made possible by Philip Sausmarez, the second son of Matthew Sausmarez. Philip Sausmarez was the first member of the family to join the Royal Navy and it was his share of the prize money from the *Cobadonga* that enabled the family to buy back Sausmarez Manor in 1748, almost two hundred years after it had first passed from their hands. Many fine houses were built on the island during the privateering era, characterized by the architectural style of five windows across the top storey and two windows on each side of the front door, making a total of nine windows.

The amount of money brought into the Bailiwick through privateering activities was phenomenal and Guernsey privateers seemed to be far more organized and successful than those of their sister isle, Jersey. It was big business and the finance industry eighteenth-century style. In retrospect the Bailiwick was lucky that the legitimately aggrieved nations (that is, the non-enemies of the British Crown) such as the Dutch, the Danish and the Ottoman Empire, did not declare war on Guernsey as the Dutch had threatened to do to the Isles of Scilly during the Civil War. If that had happened the Channel Islands might have forfeited the medieval privileges granted by King John which they enjoy to this day.

Privateering was eventually abolished in 1856 by international agreement, but many innocent foreign merchants and businessmen from countries friendly to Britain, and even from Britain itself, had been ruined by the avaricious and conscienceless behaviour of those privateers who would sell the ship's crew or press-gang them into service on ships belonging to their own country, neither of which they were legally permitted to do. Much of the time privateering was little better than a semi-legalized form of pirating, which had long been an unofficial profession in the Channel Islands. It is perhaps ironic that, having built on this dubiously acquired wealth from many countries, notably Spain, Holland and England, Guernsey today has a reputation of exclusivity and, until recently, no non-islander, including the English (to whose Crown Guernsey swears allegiance), could purchase a house on the island unless they had several million pounds in their bank account.

Chapter 11

A Sarkese Murder

c.1878

'. . . marks of strangulation had been visible upon her neck, but . . . no inquest was held . . .'

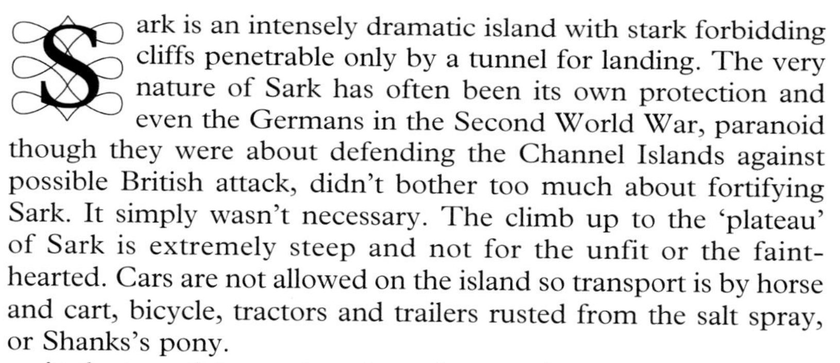

Sark is an intensely dramatic island with stark forbidding cliffs penetrable only by a tunnel for landing. The very nature of Sark has often been its own protection and even the Germans in the Second World War, paranoid though they were about defending the Channel Islands against possible British attack, didn't bother too much about fortifying Sark. It simply wasn't necessary. The climb up to the 'plateau' of Sark is extremely steep and not for the unfit or the faint-hearted. Cars are not allowed on the island so transport is by horse and cart, bicycle, tractors and trailers rusted from the salt spray, or Shanks's pony.

At the top of the road up from the quay is a crossroads flanked by branches of Barclays and the National Westminster banks, since finance on Sark, like everywhere else in the Channel Islands, is a very important industry. Sark is something of an anachronism, a feudal society in the middle of the twenty-first-century age of new technology. Until about sixty years ago the island subsisted mainly on agriculture and fishing, supplemented, as on every other Channel Island, by smuggling. Today tourism is the main industry and the island's main 'street', grandly known as The Avenue, is much given over to postcard and souvenir shops. However, one small establishment is run by a lady of certain years who wears a clean old-fashioned overall-style of apron and bakes her own very delicious pies and bread. To step into her shop is to step back in time and she is the one who, quite literally, gives visitors a taste of old Sark. At the end of The Avenue stands the small jail, looking like a neatly compacted cattleshed with a small arched roof. Sark is ruled by its Seigneur and still runs its affairs on feudal lines. Possibly the most celebrated Seigneur of Sark was a woman, Sybil Hathaway, Dame of Sark, who ruled the island

The prison on Sark, *c.*1915. Author's collection

during the Second World War and never let the Germans get the better of her.

Sark has a certain raw majestic beauty, but to live on the island requires a certain amount of backbone and character, and the place has always attracted those who regard themselves as individualists. Derrible Bay, on the south coast, is a beautiful bay divided from Dixcart Bay to the west by the Hog's Back, a steep grassy headland with lush buttercup meadows, beautiful skies, and spectacular views out to sea and to Little Sark. There are wooded valleys and hidden cottages in the hinterland of the two bays, interlaced with shady lanes and leafy dells. A pint of beer in the old stone-built pub puts most 'real ales' to shame. Time has little meaning. The roar and bustle of modern life seem light years away. There is nothing sinister here of which to be afraid, yet as the shadows gather in the dusk and moonlight filters through the trees there is a whisper, just a whisper, to suggest that one might not be completely alone.

It was to Derrible Bay that an English artist came to live in the 1870s. He wanted to paint the island, the seascapes, and the effects of the wide open skies above him. Coming from the belching chimneys and smogs of late nineteenth-century

England, Sark must have seemed to him like another world. The Channel Islands all have that special light effect common to islands and there is something compelling about the sea in all its moods. The English artist preferred to keep himself to himself, so much so that even the record of his name is not in the public domain. He rented the house known as La Tourelle which stands above Derrible Bay and there he settled down to work. He had brought a lady with him, though who she was remained a mystery and it was never quite clear if she was his wife or his girlfriend. They were not a popular couple at all with the islanders. She was frail and withdrawn; he was morose, reclusive and bad-tempered. Sometimes she was seen walking around Derrible Bay or in the lanes near the cottage, her cloak wrapped about her, almost a misty ethereal figure, her feet barely making a sound.

The two of them lived an isolated life. He had his work and it was said that she painted too. It was her misfortune to live at a time when women were not respected for their artistic or cultural abilities and she would always remain in the shadow of the brusque unsociable man with whom she lived. Gradually she became more frail and her health began to break down. It is not known if her companion ill-treated her. If he did she never sought help, but then little would have been available to her in those days, and even if it had, it is doubtful whether she would ever have dared to ask. After a few years living on the island the woman died, but it came as little surprise because of her extreme frailty. However, rumours began to circulate that she had not died a natural death. It was reported that marks of strangulation had been visible on her neck, but, despite this, no inquest was held and the Seigneur allowed her body to be buried. The Sark nurse went to La Tourelle to wash her and dress her and lay her out ready for her funeral. Few attended the service or watched her laid to rest in the small churchyard. The artist erected an elaborate cross in memory of his dear departed and left the island soon afterwards. No one was sad to see him go. However, the memorial to his lady would not remain upright and was constantly found lying flat in the grass beside her grave. Every attempt was made to fix it but to no avail and eventually it was removed altogether. Several folk claimed to have seen her ghost wandering in the lane leading to La Tourelle and the house gained a reputation for being haunted. Her apparition was also seen in the woods above the harbour by a convalescent soldier just after the First World War, although by this time four decades had elapsed since her death.

In the early 1920s the Sarkese nurse, now old and mortally ill, asked to make a confession on her deathbed. She recalled that day nearly fifty years before when she had been sent to lay out and dress the artist's dead lady. She had taken off the woman's clothes to wash her before she laid her out for her funeral. She washed the body carefully and respectfully, brushing the woman's hair back so that she could sponge the face and neck properly. It was then that she had noticed marks on the woman's neck which had been hidden by a scarf. Surprised, she had examined them carefully and there was little doubt in her mind that the poor unfortunate creature had been strangled. Mindful of the Seigneur's orders, and afraid of incurring his displeasure, and, worse still, that of the artist whom she now suspected must have killed the woman, she had been too frightened to say anything, but it had remained on her conscience ever since. When she heard the stories of the woman's ghost being seen around the house the nurse had realized that her spirit was haunting the house because she had not died a natural death. After the trouble with the memorial on the woman's grave her suspicions that the artist had killed the woman became certainty, but she was too frightened to say anything in case misfortune befell her. She begged forgiveness from God before she died and received her absolution. After all, the crime was not hers.

By this time nigh on half a century had passed since the mysterious death of the artist's lady. No one knew where he had gone when he left Sark and it was thought highly probable that he too was now dead. So the matter was laid to rest. Shortly afterwards Mr Shepard, a solicitor from Newcastle, bought La Tourelle and began extensive renovations. This seemed to offer a kind of release to the unquiet spirit for, after the alterations had been completed, the ghost seemed to fade away like the sea mists which so often surround Sark. The circumstantial evidence for the murder of this sad forgotten lady by her irascible artist husband or lover is strong, but the real truth of what happened to her in the old house up above Derrible Bay is unlikely ever to be known.

CHAPTER 12

A Crying Evil

1899–1900

'Both Mr Harris and the boy struggled and protested, but to no avail . . .'

To understand the following story it is necessary to understand the unusual and insular position of Guernsey. The Channel Islands are not actually part of England. According to both the Home and Foreign Offices they are 'a Crown Dependency'. Through a quirk of history the Islands owe allegiance to the English Crown, but not to the UK Parliament, although they must abide by Whitehall's decisions on foreign policy. However, internally, the Islands are autonomous, and can make their own domestic laws. Over the centuries this has sometimes caused outsiders bewilderment, confusion, incomprehension and outrage in turn.

In 1899 a strange and unusual case of 'kidnapping' occurred which was instigated by the law rather than someone seizing a person violently and demanding a ransom for their safe return. The 'victim' was the adopted son of the person from whom he was kidnapped and the kidnapper was his own father. In this the father was aided and abetted and physically assisted in the 'kidnapping' by the Guernsey police, although the kidnapping took place in England and not on Guernsey. The subsequent newspaper reports dubbed the case 'a crying evil', hence the title of this story.

Towards the end of 1898 an English gentleman named Luwee Harris adopted a boy in Jersey. This was done with the full consent of the boy's parents, a Mr and Mrs Maguire, who were living in reduced circumstances owing to the recent failure of their business. Subsequently the boy went to live with Mr Harris, taking his name. About two weeks after the adoption Mr Harris had the child baptized and members of the boy's blood family were present. Luwee Harris was a prosperous professional man, who fed, clothed, and housed his adopted son generously, and sent him to the High School for Boys at Colomberie on Jersey. The boy, who had not been well treated by his parents, appeared to be very content with his new circumstances. In July 1899 Mr Harris and his adopted son moved to England, preparatory to emigrating to Canada, but two months later, in September, the Maguires changed their mind and wanted the boy back. Mr Harris refused, whereupon the child was 'kidnapped' and taken to Guernsey, where his parents, having moved away from Jersey, were now living. Furious, Mr Harris took the first boat to Guernsey and lodged proceedings against the Maguires. He was warned against the wisdom of doing this by islanders who told him that 'you will get no satisfaction from this Court . . . they are muddlers . . . they are all related, and what one says, the other says', and besides Mr Harris was not an islander. This last point turned out to be the one which would hinder him the most. Luwee Harris listened to what they said and decided to ignore them because he wanted his adopted son back with him. It was a decision that was to cost him dear.

However on 22 October the boy left his parents and returned to Mr Harris of his own accord. The pair then sailed back to Weymouth. On arrival at the port the boy was detained by the Weymouth police, acting on the instructions of the Guernsey police. Mr Harris refused to release his adopted son and he was detained as well, again on the orders of the Guernsey police. An hour later the Guernsey police ordered his release but Mr Harris still refused to give up the child. The Weymouth police said that they could not release the boy without a court order, so Mr Harris consulted a solicitor, Mr A F Eaton, and instructed him to obtain a court order because he himself refused to leave his adopted child's side.

Next morning Mr Harris and his adopted son appeared before the court in Weymouth. Here it was decided that in a case such as this one neither the police nor the local justices of the peace had any right to detain either Harris or the boy and both were released. By now Mr Harris wanted his custody rights to be settled in the English High Court and so he and his adopted son remained in Weymouth to await the arrival of Mr Maguire. However, when Mr Maguire arrived he did not institute any legal proceedings but made another attempt to kidnap the child, which was foiled by the Weymouth police. Mr Maguire then telegraphed Guernsey to issue a warrant for Mr Harris's arrest.

A few days later PC Pulsford from Guernsey arrived in Weymouth with the warrant. French was still the official language of the Channel Islands so the warrant was in French and it could be neither read nor understood by Mr Harris. At this point the whole case began to descend into an unbelievable farce. Mr Harris was arrested by the Guernsey police, and handcuffed, at Upway, near Weymouth, where the warrant was not valid because the protagonists were on English soil. He was refused a Habeas Corpus application for himself and the child to be taken before a magistrate or a judge and he was refused communication with his solicitor. Mr Harris and the child were still together at this point. PC Pulsford then forcibly removed Mr Harris from the boy, who was subsequently taken away by Maguire. Both Mr Harris and the boy struggled and protested, but to no avail; and it is quite difficult to resist brute force if one is handcuffed. Mr Harris at once made another application under Habeas Corpus to be taken before a magistrate first thing next morning. Instead, that night he was put on board a steamer for Guernsey and on arrival in St Peter Port was thrown into prison. He was again refused an application for a court appearance under the terms of Habeas Corpus, because the English terms of Habeas Corpus did not apply in Guernsey. He was then charged with kidnapping and committed for trial before the Royal Court of Guernsey.

At his trial Mr Harris's defence advocate, Victor Carey, was not allowed to quote from any precedents in English law on the grounds that English law had no jurisdiction in Guernsey; despite the fact that Guernsey law had been enforced, with the use of force, on the English mainland where Mr Harris had been denied his statutory rights under English law and under Habeas Corpus. The principles of Habeas Corpus are enshrined within the English legal constitution and are dear to every English person's heart, just as Guernsey's privileges granted by King John so long ago are dear to islanders' hearts. This cut no ice with the Royal Court because English law does not have legal effect in Guernsey. However, the fact that the boy had gone and remained willingly with Mr Harris was also overlooked by the Royal Court. Consequently, to the amazement even of the islanders, Mr Harris was convicted of kidnapping and sentenced to three months in prison with hard labour. There was no appeal against the Royal Court's decision and, despite many letters of support, Luwee Harris had to serve his sentence in full. His name and reputation were besmirched and he now had a criminal record. It was a high price to pay for doing what he believed to be right.

Whatever the rights and wrongs of this case, an interesting and telling postscript can be found in the *Chronique de Jersey* for Saturday 1 December 1900. Two ladies, one aged about forty-five years old, the other around seventy, were found lying wrapped in each others' arms on the floor of a house in St Helier. They were almost dead of starvation. The son of the younger woman was found in a similar state in another room. Their family business had failed and their possessions had been sold the previous August by the local bailiff. Since then they had managed to buy food by selling their clothes, being too embarrassed and too highly principled to seek help from funds for the poor of the parish. They were sent at once to the local hospital (the equivalent of the English workhouse) just in time to save them from dying from want of food. It turned out that they were the mother, sister and nephew of Mr Maguire, who had left them to fend for themselves when he moved to Guernsey, and who had allowed Mr Harris to adopt his son before changing his mind. This incident speaks volumes about the background of the family from which the boy had tried to escape and the character of his blood father.

An integral part of this story is that Guernsey had not adopted Habeas Corpus when this 'foul deed' of kidnapping with menaces and false imprisonment took place. However, the Habeas Corpus Act, passed on 27 May 1679 and ratified by King Charles II (31 Car. 2 c. 2), states in Clause XII that the Act covers all of England and Wales, the town of Berwick-upon-Tweed (a border town of disputed ownership between England and Scotland), Jersey and Guernsey. Less than twenty years before the Act was passed Charles II had given Guernsey a royal pardon for supporting Oliver Cromwell, and not the monarchy, in the English Civil War (1640–9) and he had restored the privileges granted to them by King John in 1204. As the Islands had elected to continue to owe their allegiance to the English Crown, the King probably assumed that Guernsey would respect his wishes and adopt the Act into their constitution.

A writer of 1900 expressed his total exasperation with the Guernsey legal system when the Royal Court subsequently failed to honour a pledge to adopt the principle of Habeas Corpus, which is enshrined in English law, and gives a person the right to obtain a writ and go before a court if he or she thinks he or she is being unlawfully held or imprisoned:

promises of obedience or reformation by the Court of Guernsey . . . are of no value . . . they do nothing, and will not do anything until they are forced thereto . . . they are too exclusive and too superior in their insular prejudice, and while the people groan and complain they have no redress, and the Court goes its way unchecked, defrauding the Crown, defying the British Constitution, treating with contempt the legislative wisdom of the British Parliament, nullifying English Statute Law, usurping the jurisdiction of the English High Courts, and flouting the decisions of the High Courts. (Philippe Ahier, Letters on the case of 'A Crying Evil', *Guernsey Pamphlets, vol. IX, no. 7, pp. 20–8, 1901)*

Has Guernsey now adopted Habeas Corpus? The island, of course, is entitled to make its own internal laws without adopting English laws, but the Habeas Corpus Act of 1816, although amended in places from the original, states that 'a writ of habeas corpus . . . may be directed and run into any county palatine or cinque port, or any other privileged place within . . . England, dominion of Wales, and town of Berwick-upon-Tweed, and the Isles of Jersey, Guernsey and Man' (Habeas Corpus Act 1816: 56 Geo. 3 c. 100). However, this did not seem to apply in the case of Luwee Harris. In 2000, an article on human rights legislation commented that the Isle of Man had recently adopted Habeas Corpus but that Guernsey had not.

Today the situation seems little changed. The Greffe at the Royal Court refers enquiries about Habeas Corpus to the Law Office. The Law Office holds copies of *Halsbury's Laws* which contain Habeas Corpus and its various amendments, but Guernsey police do not seem to be aware of Habeas Corpus. In England 'every arresting officer must know and abide by the terms of Habeas Corpus' (English police officer with over twenty years' experience) and understand that he or she is legally allowed to hold a suspect for a specific time only, before he or she must take that person in front of a magistrate with either a charge to answer or a request for more time to question the suspect. The process in Guernsey may be a modified version: the Citizens Advice Bureau in St Sampson has a copy of *The Laws of Guernsey* (Dawes and Gordon, Oxford University Press, 2003), in which it is stated that if a bail application is refused then the person involved may appeal to the Bailiff; although there is no appeal against the Bailiff's decision. The confusion in many people's minds arises from the fact that, though Guernsey islanders think of themselves as English, speak English as their native tongue, and owe allegiance to Queen Elizabeth II (Queen Victoria in Mr Harris's time), their legal system and their laws are their own and, in many cases, different to those of England. This is the principle that Luwee Harris failed to grasp and it was this failure which ruined his life.

CHAPTER 13

Bewitching Guernsey

1556

'. . . in Guernsey I watched a woman burn; and in her agony the mother came upon her [and] a child was born and . . . they hurl'd it back into the fire . . .'

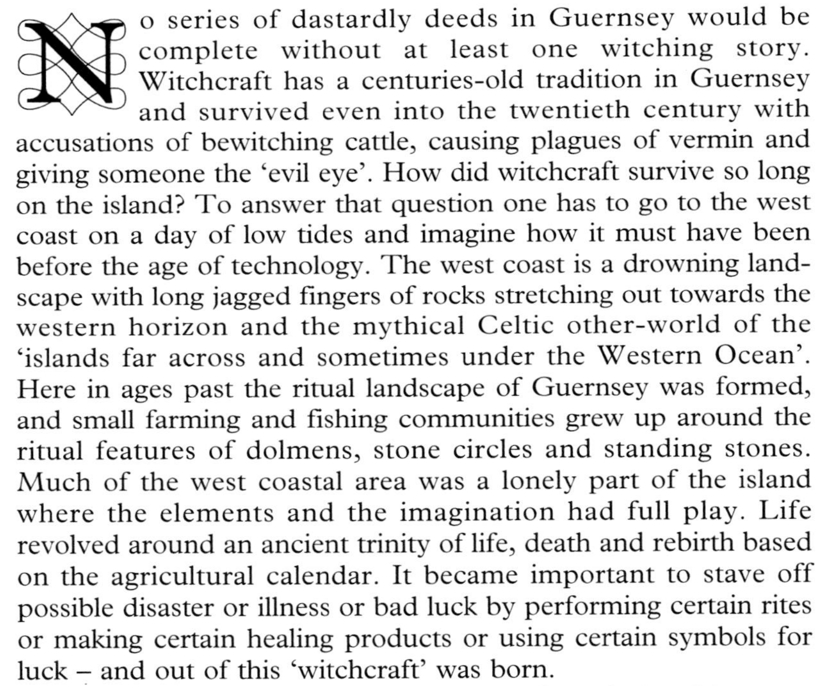

No series of dastardly deeds in Guernsey would be complete without at least one witching story. Witchcraft has a centuries-old tradition in Guernsey and survived even into the twentieth century with accusations of bewitching cattle, causing plagues of vermin and giving someone the 'evil eye'. How did witchcraft survive so long on the island? To answer that question one has to go to the west coast on a day of low tides and imagine how it must have been before the age of technology. The west coast is a drowning landscape with long jagged fingers of rocks stretching out towards the western horizon and the mythical Celtic other-world of the 'islands far across and sometimes under the Western Ocean'. Here in ages past the ritual landscape of Guernsey was formed, and small farming and fishing communities grew up around the ritual features of dolmens, stone circles and standing stones. Much of the west coastal area was a lonely part of the island where the elements and the imagination had full play. Life revolved around an ancient trinity of life, death and rebirth based on the agricultural calendar. It became important to stave off possible disaster or illness or bad luck by performing certain rites or making certain healing products or using certain symbols for luck – and out of this 'witchcraft' was born.

Over the centuries on the west coast, later isolated by poor roads, farm fields and Seigneurial woodlands, life and customs went on unchanged and unchallenged for centuries. Superstition and ancient beliefs flourished. In his novel *The Book of Ebenezer Le Page*, the Guernsey writer G B Edwards vividly describes the difficulties of travel and why the hero, Ebenezer, who lived in an old cottage at the back of Vale, did not see his lady love, Lisa

Queripel, who lived at Pleinmont, for ten years. Today the journey takes less than half an hour on the 'green and yellows' (the ultra-modern bus service). Stories abounded of witches meeting in lonely places, often on the site of a prehistoric monument. The best known of these witches' meeting places was the dolmen of Le Trepied at Catioroc between L'Erée and Perelle. It is said that each Friday night (the witches' sabbath) witches danced on the capstones in a wild frenzy, often joined by the Devil in the guise of a black goat, and screamed abuse at the Chapel of Our Lady on the island of Lihou, which is joined to L'Erée by a causeway at low tide.

Amazingly, the last trial for witchcraft on the island took place in the early years of the twentieth century (see Chapter 18, 'The Magic of Brown & Polson'). The alleged witch in question, Aimée Lake (nee Queripel), lived at St Sampson and dispensed 'charms' made of harmless everyday ingredients such as starch, baking powder and Brown & Polson's cornflour from which blancmange is made. Their power depended more on the beliefs of the superstitious people using them than anything else and similar 'charms' can be found on sale in various 'New Age' shops today, though their potency depends on the faith of both the user and the receiver. Finally a frightened and hysterical woman, whom Aimée Lake had threatened for alleged non-payment of a bill, denounced her as a witch. The hapless Mrs Lake was charged with witchcraft in January 1914. She defended herself by saying that people came to her of their own free will and asked her for help; but, possibly not helped by the fact that a distant ancestor of hers, Alechette Queripel, had been burned at the stake as a witch in 1598, and in 1624 a certain Jean Queripel had met a similar grisly end for practising witchcraft, she was found guilty and sentenced to eight days' imprisonment.

There was an acknowledged 'European witch craze' in the sixteenth and seventeenth centuries as Catholicism and Protestantism struggled for supremacy during the Reformation; but while the lighter side of witchcraft, and the practice of building 'witch ledges' into chimney stacks on Guernsey for passing witches to rest upon as they flew around the island on their broomsticks, may raise a few smiles, there is a much more cruel and sinister side to the history of witchcraft in Guernsey. During the hundred years from 1550 to 1650 over a hundred people were accused of witchcraft on the island and of these forty-five were burned for this 'heresy'. It is well worth noting that witches were almost exclusively women and their judges were exclusively men. The threat to women of being tortured and burned alive if they stepped out of line was doubtless an admirable form of control. The times were harsh and uncertain and Guernsey had the unenviable distinction of much more vicious and inhuman treatment of the larger number of witches hunted down than its sister island of Jersey. Between 1550 and 1650 there were seventy-seven witchcraft trials recorded in Guernsey, compared with sixty-six in Jersey in 175 years (1562–1736).

Alleged witches were first subjected to intimate body searches. Any small mole, birthmark or imperfection of the skin would be seen as the mark of the Devil. Beatings, torture and sexual abuse followed until a 'confession' was obtained. Historical records suggest that the Guernsey witch-hunters had more of a taste for brutality than their Jersey counterparts – even more so than the henchmen of the feared and hated English 'Witchfinder General', Matthew Hopkins. Guernsey's own 'Witchfinder General' was Amice de Carteret, Bailiff of the island from 1601 to 1630. During his period of office there were sixty-one trials for witchcraft on Guernsey as opposed to only twenty-six on Jersey. On Jersey witches found guilty at their trial were mostly sentenced to be hanged or strangled before their bodies were burnt at the stake. On Guernsey witches were condemned to be tortured and then burned alive. As if that fate wasn't terrible enough, there was one case on Guernsey that became notorious for its dreadful barbarism and sadistic cruelty even by the standards of the sixteenth century.

Three women, a mother and her two daughters, were found guilty of 'heresy' in 1556, denounced as witches and sentenced to die at the stake. Their fate is best described by Dr Heylin in his seventeenth-century *Survey*:

> *Katherine Cawches, a poor woman of St Peter Port, in Guernsey, was noted to be much absent from church, and her two daughters [Guillemine Gilbert and Perotine Massey] guilty of the same neglect. Upon this they were presented before James Amy, then dean of the island, who, finding in them that they held opinions contrary to those then allowed about the sacrament of the altar, pronounced them heretics, and condemned them to the fire. The poor women, on the other side, pleaded for themselves, that the doctrine had been taught to them in the time of King Edward [VI]; but if the queen [Mary Tudor, who succeeded Edward VI] was otherwise disposed, they were content to be of her religion. This was fair but it would not serve [the women having already been denounced as witches]; for by the dean they were delivered*

unto Helier Gosselin, then bailiff, and by him unto the fire, July 18, 1556. One of these daughters, Perotine Massey, she was called, was at that time great with child; her husband, who was a minister, having in those dangerous times fled the island; in the middle of the flames and anguish of her torments, her belly broke in sunder, and her child, a goodly boy, fell down into the fire, but was presently snatched up by one W. House, one of the by-standers [the surgeon at Castle Cornet]. Upon the noise of this strange incident, the cruel bailiff returned [and] commanded that the poor infant must be cast once again into the flames; which was accordingly performed; and so that pretty babe was born a martyr, and added to the number of holy innocents.

Medical opinion says that it is possible for a birth to take place under such circumstances and there is another recorded case from Madagascar in the nineteenth century. The nineteenth-century romantic poet, Alfred, Lord Tennyson, was so shocked and horrified by the story that he immortalized it in his play *Queen Mary* (Act V, Scene IV):

Sir, in Guernsey
I watch'd a woman burn; and in her agony
The mother came upon her – a child was born –
And, Sir, they hurl'd it back into the fire,
That, being baptized in fire, the babe
Might be in fire forever. Ah, good neighbour,
There should be something fierier than fire
To yield them their deserts.

Tennyson's sentiments are echoed by most of us and the States have put a memorial plaque on the wall halfway up Tower Hill steps which commemorates the site of this most dastardly of deeds. Today Tower Hill is a strangely peaceful place with no echoes of the searing screams of terror, pain and torment from those condemned to die in such a hellish way. There are no ghosts haunting the steep flight of steps leading from a quiet shopping street up to the crooked older houses clustered together on the top of Tower Hill. The burnings took place at the foot of Tower Hill and legend has it that the area of the steps was known as Le Val de Misère, the Vale of Misery, because it was the last walk of those condemned to die without mercy at the stake.

This cruel torture continued well into the seventeenth century, and, unbelievably, the burning of whole families occurred at least twice more in Guernsey. On 18 August 1617 Jeanne de Callais

Plaque commemorating the burning of three alleged witches, one of whom gave birth as she died. The author

(née Guignon) and two of her children were taken to Tower Hill and 'hanged and burnt after being put to the question'. By now of course the religious elements had changed. Katherine Cawches and her daughters had been burned for displeasing a Catholic Queen with their Protestant ways. Jeanne de Callais and her children were burned for displeasing a Protestant monarch with their Catholic ways. Since the Catholic Queen, Mary Tudor, died in

The re-enaction of the tragedy of Katherine Cawches and her two daughters by Guernsey Living History to mark the 450th anniversary of their execution on 18th July 1556 on Tower Hill St Peter Port Guernsey. The author

1558, it was decreed that England should never have another Catholic monarch, and constitutionally the country still cannot do so. The burning of Jeanne de Callais and her family was followed five years later in 1622 by the hanging and burning of Collette Tourgis (née de l'Estac). Her husband, Thomas, and daughter, Jeanne, were burned alive on 17 October that year. This case was quite unusual in that a man was burned to death for witchcraft.

Does witchcraft still play a part in twenty-first-century life, an age of mobile phones and instant technology which can connect places across the world in seconds? The surprising answer is yes, because, although most of us won't admit it, superstition is alive and well, and the spiritual need ingrained in the human race all over the globe since time immemorial for some sort of ritual at significant times of our lives, is part of our make-up. Herbal remedies, widely used in former centuries by 'witches' to cure various ailments, have become popular and fashionable; and the explanation of dreams (with which Aimée Lake was also charged, as further proof of her witchcraft) is an accepted part of modern psychology practices. The 'occult sections' of bookshops are growing and there is an increasing number of covens. Many of the members consider themselves 'white witches', but there is also some evidence of the practice of the black arts or devil worship. These include small animals which have clearly been killed for sacrifice, and the number 666 (said to be much favoured by his Satanic majesty) can be found crudely painted on the walls of more than one wartime German bunker on the island. Witchcraft, it would seem, has never lost its fascination, but it is to be fervently hoped that the terrible deeds committed against the witches of earlier centuries are never ever witnessed again.

Chapter 14

The Grave on Herm Sands

1832

'. . . the question is . . . why are two seemingly unrelated people sharing a grave?'

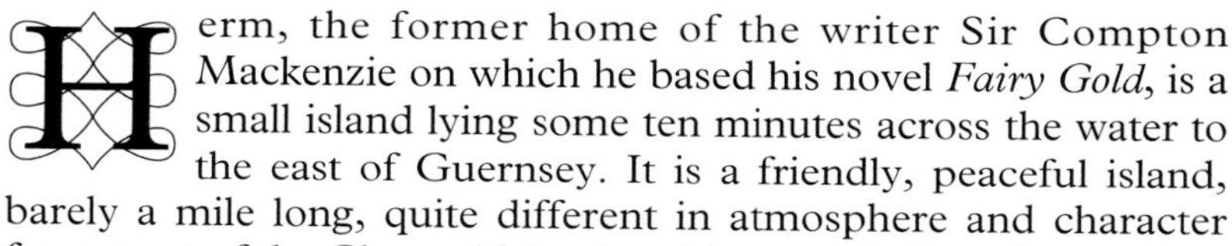

Herm, the former home of the writer Sir Compton Mackenzie on which he based his novel *Fairy Gold*, is a small island lying some ten minutes across the water to the east of Guernsey. It is a friendly, peaceful island, barely a mile long, quite different in atmosphere and character from most of the Channel Islands, with a population of some sixty to seventy people. The south of the island is full of rocky cliffs; the northern part is flatter. There are a number of ancient graves and ritual monuments, although many were destroyed by the quarrying activities of the nineteenth century. The famed Shell Beach runs along the north-eastern coast, so named for the thousands of tiny different-coloured shells which can be found here lying along the half mile or so of golden sands.

The White House (the only characteristic it shares with the same-named home of the American President is its colour) stands above the harbour, a kind of division between the low ground to the north and the high ground to the south. In the gardens stand what appears to be a large stone beehive, but it is actually the world's smallest jail, just large enough for a couple of prisoners to lie down. It was in The White House that Prince Blücher, a Prussian prince, made his home at the end of the nineteenth century. He and his family fell in love with Herm. They farmed the land, introduced wallabies to the island, and wandered the Shell Beach marvelling at the beautiful tiny shells lying sparkling on the sand. After the outbreak of the Great War in 1914 the Prince was given two months to leave the home he loved. In vain he protested that he was a naturalized British citizen but to no avail. He left in 1915 after twenty-six years on his beloved island. When the war was over his family were given permission to return

The tiny jail on Herm, 2005. This 'beehive' is said to be the smallest jail in the world. The author

but it was too late for Prince Blücher. He had died of a broken heart in 1916.

The Fisherman's Path leads from the Mermaid's Tavern around the western side of the island. Sir Compton Mackenzie loved this part of the island and walked here often, but one evening while out for a stroll at dusk he suddenly felt surrounded by what were described as 'elemental forces'. Thoroughly unnerved, he turned and fled home. He was shaken by the experience and vowed not to repeat it. Near to where Sir Compton had his unnerving experience lies the Island Cemetery at the end of the Fisherman's Path. It must count as one of the smallest cemeteries in the world, since it contains only two people and just one grave. There is an inscription with names and dates on the headstone but no one knows anything about those who lie in the grave or how they came to be there.

The simple inscription reads:

In Memory of
K W Conden aged 2 years
and
R Mansfield aged 33 years
Died April 1832
Rest in Peace

Perhaps it is the grave of a mother and her young child – but then why should they be lying here by the seashore and not in the

A mysterious gravestone on the eastern coast of Herm. The author

consecrated ground of the church, and why should they have different names? How did they die and where are the loving inscriptions? Could they be a nursemaid and her young charge, or perhaps a father and his small child? Whatever the combination, it does not answer the questions. Even if the adult had committed suicide and so could not (at that time) be buried in consecrated ground, suicide could not have been the cause of death of a two-year-old child.

However, technological advances in the twentieth century meant that the gravestone, by now rather worn and weathered in places, could be examined under more scientific conditions. Photographic magnification of almost 200 times revealed traces of another figure 2 beside the visible 2, so that K W Conden was not a child of two but a young adult of twenty-two. Why was the second figure 2 so worn? It almost looks as though it was carefully and gently erased from the stone, but why should someone go to all that trouble?

Were the two dead people friends, then, or cousins? The initials do not reveal even if they were male or female; although the mere use of initials (especially at that period of history) and the fact that more masculine than feminine Christian names begin with K and R suggest that the incumbents of the grave may have been male.

The rest of the inscription is reasonably legible, although 1832 could be 1852. These people should be so easy to trace and identify, but they are not. They are not known on Herm. There are no cases reported in the newspapers around the relevant dates. The burial registers do not give the answers. It is not known whether they were male or female. The lack of personal detail, such as full Christian name and date of birth, and any kind of loving remembrance, suggests that they were not local. There still remains the mystery of why they were buried on the seashore, since even strangers were accorded full Christian burial. If there was no room in the local churchyard they would have been taken to Guernsey just ten minutes away across the water.

One story was that the two dead people were victims of cholera, in which case there should have been some medical record, as cholera was a reportable and highly infectious disease. There was an outbreak on Guernsey in 1899 but this date is several decades after the grave was dug. They could of course have come in on a ship but then that ship should have been quarantined and anyone

Jethou (twentieth century), showing the turbulent waters where two friends drowned after their boat sank in 1858. Reproduced by kind permission of the Priaulx Library, St Peter Port, Guernsey

who was sick would probably have been sent to Jethou, Herm's small 'off-island'.

Another story is that the bodies were those of two men who were friends and who drowned in the narrow but turbulent passage between Herm and Jethou in 1858, but again the date is wrong. Yet another theory was that the grave was that of two men who drowned when the *Ranger*, a ship owned by a brandy smuggler, sank off Herm in 1873. Once more the date is too late and such an incident would have been reported in the newspapers. Drownings and shipwrecks would have been hot topics of conversation and very difficult to hide.

The final burning question is why are these two seemingly unrelated people sharing a grave? Why only the one grave and why were they buried on the seashore? That could happen to shipwreck victims but it was always a temporary measure. Were these unknown people criminals or murderers? Trials and executions were carried out on Guernsey, however, so why would they have been buried on Herm? Suicides? Why two together? Were they star-crossed lovers who saw that the only way ever to be together was in death? Again there seems to be no supporting evidence of any kind. Official records show no trace of two men or women with these names who died or were killed or who committed suicide in the nineteenth century on Herm; but yet they must have been somebody's children. Someone somewhere must have known who they were. As Paul Newman so memorably said in *Butch Cassidy and the Sundance Kid*, on continually failing to throw the pursuing posse off their trail, 'Who are those guys?'

Chapter 15

A Dastardly Tragedy

1912

'. . . in the end the law preferred to allow the islanders their belief that dark powers had killed John Robert . . .'

Guernsey on the eve of the First World War (1914–18) was still essentially rural, despite the number of quarries on the island (over two hundred at this time). Shipbuilding in St Peter Port had declined as iron steamships took over from wooden sailing ships. The finance and tourist industries lay in the future. Farmers grew potatoes and tomatoes and the time-honoured crop of parsnips, which had been grown for centuries in large enough quantities to merit a festival when the parsnip seeds were first sown in freshly tilled soil. Appropriately enough, given Guernsey's folklore beliefs in witches and devils, parsnips were believed to be a favourite food of the Devil. Everyone helped everyone else at sowing and harvesting times, and in the rural parishes most people knew most other people. French, the official language until 1904, had been replaced by English, but most people continued to speak the old Anglo-Norman patois, a curious mixture of French and English which had developed over the centuries. The French franc was still the official currency. Belief in the supernatural was still very strong and the population was incredibly superstitious. People were terrified of evil spirits which they seemed to believe inhabited the island just waiting to pounce on the unwary and bring them misfortune. Local witches did a roaring trade in spells and potions and herbal remedies, although witchcraft was an imprisonable offence in Guernsey until after the war. So widespread were such beliefs that they permeated every level of society, which goes some way towards explaining the events that occurred in St Sampson and L'Islet in the late autumn of 1912.

'Dastardly Tragedy'. So ran the headline of *The Star* for 12 November 1912, some two months after the sinking of the *Titanic*, which had been a talking point for weeks. A 'dastardly tragedy' had occurred which was to become part of a reign of terror, caused, most said, by an 'evil spirit' released by the recent opening of an ancient tomb. The stuff of legend, as 'foul deeds' go.

John Brache Robert was sixty-three years of age. A farmer and fruit grower, he lived in Les Capelles, a large house at Les Canus in the parish of St Sampson. Mr Robert was a bachelor and had sold or rented out most of his estate. He was a man of regular habits who usually retired to bed early and it was his custom to spend each Saturday evening with one of his relatives, a man called Nicholas Robert, who lived at Les Pièces about ten minutes' walk away. Saturday 9 December was no exception and Mr Robert left Nicholas's home at about 8.30 in the evening.

The next morning, at about nine o'clock, his neighbours, the Olliviers, noticed that Mr Robert's curtains were still drawn. This was highly unusual, since he was an early riser. It being a Sunday, they did not wish to intrude upon him, but when it got to 10.30 and the curtains were still drawn, Mr Gabriel, another close neighbour, entered the house through the 'lean-to' conservatory at the rear of the premises to see if Mr Robert was ill. The conservatory had a connecting door to the house and was never locked except when Mr Robert retired to bed. As he entered the conservatory Mr Gabriel came to a sudden shocked halt. John Robert 'lay quite dead face downward on the floor in a pool of blood'.

Constables Robilliard and Ogier were summoned at once and they immediately rang for Dr Joseph. The doctor gave the corpse a brief examination and then pronounced that Mr Robert had been dead for some hours due to 'five frightful wounds which had been inflicted on the forehead, top, side and back of the head'. Two deep wounds on the forehead were two inches wide and penetrated the bone. Mr Robert had been wearing a peaked cap and the murder weapon had penetrated right through the peak and driven it into the wound. There was also a large wound on the top of the head and at the side; but the back of the head was completely smashed in. Mr Robert's 'neck shawl' was 'saturated with blood'.

By 12.30 the body had been thoroughly examined and was removed to the bedroom to be laid out. The police had made a cursory search of the house but found little of interest. There was momentary excitement when a piece of rope was discovered beneath the mattress on his bed but it was obvious from the condition of the flattened rope that it had been there for some time and was nothing but an old piece of rope. There was more excitement when a letter in a strange hand arrived from France, and rumours abounded. However, the letter had simply been delivered to the wrong address. Although these were false clues and had no bearing on the crime, they were mentioned in the press two months later in an effort to revive flagging interest in the murder.

A reward of £100 was offered for information about the crime but no one came forward. This was considered a bit unusual, given the Guernseyman's love of money, but the police had other things to think about. There had been an unprecedented spate of attempted robberies and assaults. A St Andrew's Church chorister was beaten up. Robberies took place in the Talbot Valley, St Clair on Vale Road and in several places around St Sampson. There was an attempted rape reported at Câstel. The murder of Mr Robert seemed to be a culmination of these events.

Local residents worked themselves up into a thoroughly frightened community living on the edge of fear, and 'unsuspicious security was replaced by bolted doors and windows'. Many isolated homes lay along the lonely and badly lit roads around St Sampson, L'Islet and L'Ancresse and their residents imposed an unofficial curfew on themselves. Women left on their own, whose menfolk were away all day and often most of the evening, were especially nervous. There was criticism of the States for deciding not to install street lighting on many roads and a call for temporary constables to be sworn in. *The Star* ran hysterical headlines throughout December: 'Alarm in Northern Parishes', 'Terrified Women', 'Reign of Terror'. Then, in the middle of all this, Clifford Nicolle, a St Sampson man, disappeared without trace.

The failure of the police to find out who or what lay behind this sudden crime wave led the superstitious and panic-stricken islanders to put forward their own explanation: 'a few weeks ago a dolmen was opened at L'Islet and . . . the evil spirit . . . has escaped from its imprisonment in the tomb', wrote *The Star* reporter. The opening of the dolmen had attracted much interest and large numbers of people visited the site. Such an interest in archaeology might be considered unusual for an isolated farming and fishing community at such a time, but there had been unease for several weeks over the redevelopment taking place at L'Islet which had resulted in the dolmen being destroyed to make way for the building of some new cottages. It was considered very unlucky and a sacrilege to disturb the ancient dead and there were those who shook their heads and muttered darkly that what had happened recently in the community was only to be expected and that there might be worse to come.

Certainly the dolmen was an unusual one. It was flanked on either side by cist burials surrounded by circles of eleven stones, a number much favoured by his Satanic majesty. The site stood close to the edge of L'Ancresse Common, which had its own quota of prehistoric tombs and one of the oldest settlement sites in Europe. There were a number of standing stones in the area as well and these had been worshipped well into historic times. For a population steeped in a belief in witchcraft and the 'old ways', opening such a dolmen brought the kind of foreboding felt by the ordinary Egyptian people when a Pharaoh's tomb was opened. An article in the *Transactions of the Société Guernesiaise* for 1915 stated that dolmens were said to 'have the same powers and wrath as pyramids', which only served to confirm what the islanders thought they knew already. The opening of the tomb at L'Islet had released an 'evil spirit' which had gone on the rampage, attacking and plundering the parish that had allowed the tomb to be desecrated in this way, and the rampage had finally culminated in a murderous attack on John Robert, the 'evil spirit' smashing his head to pieces in its rage.

A few weeks later, in the middle of February 1913, there was an outbreak of diphtheria and once again this was attributed to the curse of the tomb. Islanders refused to take any precautionary

Dolmen at L'Islet, 1912, from which 'an evil spirit' is said to have escaped.
Courtesy of States Archives Service

measures and Dr Carruthers, a local physician, criticized his patients in a fit of frustration because

> *it is still believed in Guernsey that the infectivity of diseases like diphtheria and scarlet fever is due to witchcraft or overlooking or the opening up of cromlechs . . . against which it is useless to fight.*

The crime wave continued for several months, somewhat swamping the murder inquiry. The police, overstretched and undermanned, were kept busy. The reward offered for information failed to concentrate the islanders' minds on the case because they were under attack from both the threat of diphtheria and the fear of violence. Personal safety for themselves and their loved ones was uppermost in everyone's mind. John Robert was dead, buried and forgotten.

Forensic science would doubtless have solved the case fairly quickly but even though forensics were not available to the police in 1913, any avid reader of the Sherlock Holmes novels, which were very popular at the time, could have put forward plausible theories for a murder which was destined to remain unsolved. The answer to it lay within the island community. The time of the murder was entered in the Register of Deaths as nine o'clock on the Saturday evening, half an hour after the victim had left Nicholas Robert's house. So someone had either followed John Robert home or had lain in wait for him, knowing his regular habits. It was not a passing stranger who had attacked him so viciously, but someone with a bitter personal hatred of him. He had sold or rented out most of his estate and there was a strong possibility that the murderer was either a tenant with a grudge or a relative who felt that a family inheritance was being squandered.

Records of the police investigation appear not to have survived, so it is not known if Nicholas Robert or any other members of the family were interviewed. An inquest was held into John Robert's death but the word 'vide' appears next to the word 'inquest' in the Register of Deaths. A French dictionary gives the meaning of 'vide' as 'void'. Details of the inquest were not published and there is an embargo for a hundred years on the release of inquest papers, so no information will be publicly available until 2012. There was a virtual news black-out on the story. Murders were quite rare on the islands and other murder cases received detailed coverage but this newspaper story was remarkable for the scarcity of its detail. And it seems likely that if anyone had known anything, someone would have said something. No one did.

The fact that no one came forward with any information is

strange, for within the tightly knit community it must have been known, or at least strongly suspected, who was responsible for the murder of John Robert. Mr Robert may have had plans to dispose of further portions of his estates which would have greatly displeased other members of the family and possibly alienated tenants who would have to move. Also, as Robert Wilson found to his cost (see Chapter 28, 'Pictures on a Gravestone'), strangers were very quickly noted in Guernsey, even with immigrant workers and visiting regiments on the island. In modern terminology, it was almost certainly 'an inside job' or done by someone with 'inside information'.

The disappearance of Clifford Nicolle was finally noted but no connections were made. A newspaper report in early March said that Clifford Nicolle had probably sailed out of Guernsey on a St Sampson steamer in the first week of February without telling anyone. On 29 and 30 January, just days before, *The Star* had carried reports about new clues being found in the murder case of John Robert. Though it is uncertain if Nicolle had any connection to John Robert, he came from the same parish and, as he lived quite close to Mr Robert, he would almost certainly have known him. Why should Nicolle suddenly disappear without telling anyone? *The Star* showed little interest nor, it seems, did anyone else. If Clifford Nicolle had been involved, how easy it would have been for him to dispose of any evidence once he was at sea. However, as Sherlock Holmes might have said, 'All circumstantial, my dear Watson', and the real truth about who killed John Robert will now probably never be known. It seems as though, in the end, the law preferred to allow the islanders their belief that dark powers had killed John Robert and that he was murdered by 'someone or something unknown'.

CHAPTER 16

Escape from Death

1643

'. . . had they "delayed only half an hour longer, we had all three been hanged".'

Castle Cornet, said to have been named after a local family, was built of forbidding grey granite on a former tidal island in 1204 for the defence of Guernsey after King John had lost Normandy to the French. The early castle was of an archetypal style with walls, a ditch and a drawbridge surrounding a central square tower, a round tower and a chapel. By the time of Henry VIII the donjon (keep) and barbican (outer defensive passage) had been added. The 'angled bastion'

Castle Cornet, St Peter Port. The castle was built in 1204. The author

was added by engineer Paul Ivy during the reign of Queen Elizabeth I. Island governors lived in the castle until 1672 and it was also used as a prison. The completion of Fort George in the early 1800s somewhat superseded Castle Cornet and many of the militia were moved. Today the castle is joined to the Guernsey mainland by a permanent causeway and forms one of the breakwaters for St Peter Port.

Like all castles, Castle Cornet has its share of romantic stories. One of the most well known comes from the time of the English Civil War (1640–49). As the Channel Islands historically owe allegiance to the English Crown, it was naturally expected that the Islands would side with the Royalists during the Civil War. This happened with all the Channel Islands except for Guernsey, which did its own thing and sided with the Parliamentarians. This was mainly due to a very unpopular late Tudor administrator of the island and an unsympathetic governor of Guernsey when the Civil War began. It was a situation which caused considerable embarrassment in certain quarters, and the determination to do something to resolve the problem and restore Guernsey to the Royalist cause resulted in one of the best stories of courage in the history of the island.

Running with difficulty across the wet sands in the cold December evening, the three men could see the shores of the island so tantalizingly close. Cannon balls and grapeshot flashed from the castle and showered down around them but miraculously none of them was hit. The congregation from the local church ran into the streets, alerted by the noise and by the good tidings of their escape. As they reached dry land each man fell to his knees and, surrounded by well-wishers crying with joy, gave thanks to God for their extraordinary deliverance from their judicial would-be murderers.

It is a story well worthy of the *Boys' Own* version of dungeons and dragons – or Cavaliers and Roundheads, as this story happened during the Civil War. The king, Charles I, fearing 'the ill spirit which had brought woe upon the kingdom', was 'determined to maintain his rights' over Guernsey which, though owing allegiance to the English Crown but not the English Parliament, supported the Parliamentarians, unlike Jersey which had remained Royalist. The Lieutenant Governor of Guernsey, Sir Peter Osborne, was a Royalist and Cromwell ordered his arrest early in 1643. When this was not done, Parliament dissolved the Royal Court of Guernsey and appointed twelve commissioners to govern the island, each taking turns to be Bailiff for one month. Sir Peter retreated to Castle Cornet, which was then besieged.

In an attempt to break this deadlock and resolve the situation, Captain Bowden sailed from England and anchored off Fermain Bay on 23 October 1643. He sent a boat ashore with a letter requesting three of the commissioners, Peter de Beauvoir des Granges, James de Havilland (an ancestor in the family of actress Olivia de Havilland and her sister, Joan Fontaine, also an actress), and Peter Carey to join him on board for important discussions. However, when they arrived on board the three commissioners found that Captain Bowden had switched his allegiance from Parliament to King. Consequently they were kidnapped, arrested, taken straight to Castle Cornet and 'lodged under the lower ditch, in one of the deepest dungeons; a place so subterranean and humid, that our hair became wet, and from whence we were unable to see light but through the key-hole'.

Peter Carey afterwards wrote an account of their incarceration and subsequent escape. The first night, 'three candles were given to us to last through the night, together with three old pillows and a tattered coverlid, filled with vermin', but the next day they were moved into an apartment which had a small window that faced north-east and 'a quantity of wet match'. Match is a lightly twisted hemp rope which has been soaked in a mixture of water and wood ash. It is used for firing cannon. For the next four nights they slept on the ground before being given 'a bedstead, matrass, coverlid and sheets'. Carey also describes the food they are given in great detail: 'bacon, pease, two biscuits, and two quarts of beer . . . pease soup . . . two small whitings . . . with a little butter congealed from excessive cold . . . oat-meal and water boiled into pottage [broth]'. The food gets progressively worse: 'pease germinating, and rotten bacon . . . impossible to eat . . . boiled wheat with stinking grease', and he is outraged when the beer ration ceases and they were allowed only a pint of red wine per day between them. At this point James de Havilland proposed trying to make an escape.

On Thursday 23 November, exactly one month after their imprisonment began, the three men started to cut the floor with their knives, 'working at it about three hours a day, one among us always being on watch while the other two laboured'. By Monday 27th, they had completed their cutting of the floor, replacing the pieces so well that 'our keeper [Nicholas Ainguer] could not perceive it when he brought us our food'. However, on the morning of Sunday 3 December, 'the weather being extraordinarily serene', two Royalist ships approached the Castle and 'Mr de Sausmarez . . . arrived about midday at the Castle'. Fearing that Guernsey was about to fall into Royalist hands, 'we all three wept bitterly'.

As they ate their dinner that day, Peter des Granges suggested escaping by the tower gate. At first the others were reluctant because of the dangers, but they finally agreed it would be worse to remain, and after dinner 'determined to hazard it . . . we . . . took our cords of match, and attaching one to a pillar which was in the middle of our room, and placing the end through the hole we had made, we slipped into the room beneath'. There James de Havilland providentially found an iron bar which he used to wrench off the cramp iron lock of the door as the church bells finished ringing for evening prayers. The look-out, Peter des Granges, then saw their keeper, Nicholas Ainguer, coming towards them with his head bent so they retreated back into the room for about a quarter of an hour.

Then 'we sallied forth anew, and finding the road clear to the first cannon, facing the west, where, having fastened our match, and Mr des Granges being the first who was about to let himself down, we discovered above, three persons who were on guard. This made us hastily detach our match'. The other two were then for abandoning the attempt and returning to their room; but Peter Carey refused to give up and insisted they went round to the south side of the tower. As it happened, by great good fortune, the guards there had sneaked off to a drinking house by the porter's garden and the three men were able to scale the first and second walls without being seen. They ran along the sea side of the wall without anyone challenging them until they reached the 'neck of the castle, where John Chamberlain then was, on his post, who observed us, and immediately cried out fire, fire, the prisoners are running away'. They ran for their lives as 'they directly discharged cannon at us, one charged with large balls, the other with grapeshot, which fell all around us without wounding us, praise be to God', and, amazingly, reached the mainland of Guernsey without any injury to themselves at all, 'for which, may God be eternally blessed'.

Shortly afterwards the three ex-prisoners learned that in fact someone had seen them fleeing round the castle, 'a young Norman gentleman, who saw us flying, and thinking it was his cousin, with two others, and were escaping, was silent; and thus we were undiscovered'. Carey, de Havilland and des Granges also learned that an order had been brought from the king that very morning for their execution and that had they 'delayed only half an hour longer, we had all three been hanged'.

Chapter 17

Le Trepied

Late twentieth century

'. . . Dana could see nothing, hear nothing, touch nothing, smell nothing, but it was there . . . and it didn't want her there . . .'

This is an unusual but true story, vouched for by independent witnesses and medical sources, told about a lady on Guernsey identified only as Dana. It involves most of the mystic elements which have been so much a part of Guernsey life over the centuries and certainly involves foul deeds of past and present centuries, if not actual suspicious deaths. Those that there were, if indeed they occurred, will have been carefully concealed. It is quite creepy and because it has broken the rules of not writing about foul deeds which are recent (that is, twentieth century) care has been taken to disguise personal identification details. It is written as Dana tells it and makes a thought-provoking addition to this collection of stories of foul deeds.

In 1986 Guernseyman Peter Girard wrote of Le Catioroc in his excellent miscellany on Guernsey's history. He described the place as 'a fascinating patchwork of history', with ancient monuments, an eighteenth-century watch-house, a Napoleonic battery, German bunker fortifications and dark tales of witches and smugglers. Legend says that on Friday nights, their sabbath, the witches used to dance there at Le Trepied, which is a Neolithic dolmen belonging to the ritual landscape of an old golden land. Sometimes, it was said, the Devil himself, dressed in black fur, maybe in the form of a goat or a werewolf, would sit on the capstones of Le Trepied as the witches whirled around him in a frenzy, hurling abuse at the chapel on the nearby island of Lihou dedicated to Notre Dame, or Marie de Lihou, as she is called locally. According to the renowned exiled French writer, Victor Hugo, Le Trepied was haunted by the cries of the women waiting for their demon lover. The Devil was also said to take the guise of a black dog and lanes in the area were reputed to be haunted by a

The countryside of Le Trepied, *c.*1920. Author's collection

large black hound which was widely believed to be a portent of an impending death. In legend Heroguiazes, the Queen of Hell, led the orgies which took place there on the witches' sabbaths. She was 'identified with Hero-dias who was responsible for the death of John the Baptist and condemned to dance forever around the world in storm and whirlwind'. No one from the Perelle, L'Erée or Rocquaine districts would go near the place on Friday nights. Mr Girard ended his chapter on Le Trepied: 'Fortunately the evil reputation of the area has been dispelled and no one need hesitate to visit Le Catioroc on a Friday night.'

Great! Dana thought as she put Mr Girard's book down. Le Trepied is a beautiful spot and he'd made her want to visit it again. She decided that she would watch the sunset from there on Midsummer Day. Midsummer Day was a great festival for witches and this year it fell on a Friday – but, hey, this was the twentieth century, and stories like that belong to the past. Don't they? Anyway, hadn't Mr Girard said that everything was OK now? Perhaps she should have remembered from her archaeological training that there is always a grain of truth in folklore.

Midsummer Day evening on the West Coast was not at all what

Midsummer Day evenings should be in old golden lands. It was grey. Grey sky, grey sea, grey light, grey atmosphere, and very quiet. You could almost hear the silence. Dana left the bus at L'Erée by Le Creux es Faies, a chamber tomb beneath a large earthen mound near Le Trepied, one of the places where the fairies are said to enter Guernsey from their fairy world. She was going to do this properly but she felt very alone as the bus pulled away and disappeared around the coast to Perelle.

She'd been in Le Creux es Faies before but tonight the dark mouth of the tomb didn't seem very inviting. Come on, she thought, it had been used as a simple cattle shelter for decades before being restored. Scores of people, tending their animals, must have passed safely in and out of the tomb over the years; but had any of them ever entered it on Midsummer Day evening? Dana would never know. In any case she had forgotten to bring a torch and sensibly told herself that it would be stupid to go stumbling around in the gloom. The truth was that nothing would have made her enter the tomb that evening. Some deeper instinct had kicked in and she turned away, trying hard to ignore the fact that

The tomb of Le Trepied at Le Catioroc where the Devil was said to dance with witches and when Dana had her midsummer eve experience. The author

something or someone seemed to be doing a lot of rustling in the thicket of vegetation which partially covers the mound of Le Creux es Faies. Fairies were supposed to be the kindly little creatures half remembered from childhood stories, but the Guernsey fairies seemed nightmarishly different.

According to local folklore, long ago Le Grand Colin, the fairy king, had visited Guernsey and while he was there he had fallen deeply in love with a beautiful Guernsey girl. She finally agreed to return with him to his fairy kingdom and become his queen. Le Grand Colin's fairy subjects were impressed with the beauty of their new queen and determined to take Guernsey wives for themselves. One night the fairy men swarmed from the similarly named Le Creux aux Féas, a cave at nearby Vazon, and fought and killed all the Guernsey men so that they could marry the pretty Guernsey girls. Meanwhile Le Petit Colin, the future fairy king, had been born to Le Grand Colin and his beautiful mortal wife. However, tragedy struck and the lady died in childbirth. According to legend Le Petit Colin, part mortal, part fairy, was found as a tiny baby lying beside his dead mother in Le Creux es Faies at L'Erée. He was brought up on the island by a Guernsey mortal named Lisabeau, and remained with her, until his father, the old fairy king, Le Grand Colin, died. As he grew to manhood Le Petit Colin worked as a servant for a man named Thomas Dumaresq. Le Rocque où le Cocq Chante stands on the highest point overlooking Vazon Bay and it was said that the fairies used to dance around it on Friday nights. Legend also says that 'from this hill issued the voice bidding Thomas Dumaresq to tell his faerie serving man, "Le Petit Colin", of the death of his father, "Le Grand Colin", the king of the faeries'. When he heard the news 'Le Petit Colin' tearfully told Lisabeau that he must leave her to return to the fairy world and that they would never see each other again.

The dusk got steadily greyer as Dana walked along the coastal path from L'Erée to Le Catioroc. There was no birdsong, no sounds at all except for the waves breaking on the shore and the scrabbling of a dog, desperate to get back into his owner's car. Maybe his deeper instincts had kicked in as well. Le Catioroc was as grey as everything else but it seemed peaceful enough. No witches, no wild dancing, no wicked man in black fur sitting on the ancient tomb of Le Trepied. Just grey stones in the grey light of a grey evening looking out on a grey sea. So Mr Girard was right. There was nothing evil there any more, nothing of which to be afraid and, hey, this was the twentieth century and stories like that belonged to the past. Didn't they?

The earliest mention of the Le Trepied dolmen tomb in connection with witchcraft was in 1534 but by the seventeenth century it had become infamous as the chief midnight sabbath haunt of the witches on the island. The tomb itself dated back to the Neolithic period, the time of Stonehenge, when Britain was part of a ritual landscape characterized by stone circles, standing stones, henges and cursii (parallel earthen banks running across the landscape). In 1839–40 the dolmen had been excavated by the renowned Guernsey archaeologist, F C Lukis, and the grave goods he found were placed in the local museum. Almost a hundred years later, in 1937, someone lit a fire in the chamber of Le Trepied which caused the northernmost capstone to collapse. Dana didn't know whether that had been a part of some sacrificial ritual.

For nearly a thousand years the Church had recognized that Le Trepied somehow had deep mystical connotations and they tried to contain its influence by surrounding the place with two chapels and three crosses. The chapels stood on the offshore islands of Lihou, at whose patron saint, Marie de Lihou, the witches screamed abuse, and Dom Hue, north of La Brêche de l'Angulaire. La Croix de St Martins stood on the rocky shore below Le Trepied, opposite the chapel of Dom Hue; La Croix de Lihou stood on the highest point of the hill west of Le Creux es Faies; and La Croix at Les Adams stood just south of La Longue Rocque de Claire Mare. Dana had wondered why it was so surrounded with Christian features. Could these stories that she had heard be true?

As she reached the tomb Dana could see nothing, hear nothing, touch nothing, smell nothing, but it was there. Something – invisible, intangible, but she could sense it, feel it, and it didn't want her there. There was a stabbing pain above her right eye and her stomach felt as though a weight was dragging it down. The place was beginning to feel very creepy and unwelcoming, bringing with it a real sense of foreboding, even fear. Dana wasn't going to argue with whatever it was so she turned and, resisting the impulse to run in the treacherous dusky half-light, walked rapidly back down the hill towards the sea. As she drew level with the old German bunker close to the road Dana felt lots of tight tingling sensations as though she'd been pushed into an electrical force field, and then suddenly she was clear of it. She felt completely drained but the pain in her head had gone and her stomach was no longer dragging, although it felt sore. She was trembling as she crossed the road and sat down on the sea wall to wait for the bus home. An echo sounded, as though of distant laughter, and all the time she had the sensation of being watched, although there was no one in sight. At one point Dana thought she was going to faint, grabbing the sea wall in desperation and trying not to hear that faint mocking laughter. Had there, she wondered, once been living people sacrificed on the stones of Le Catioroc?

When the bus finally arrived with its bright yellow headlights, and the means of escape it offered, her relief was palpable. Dana paid her fare and stumbled into a seat with indecent haste. That night she slept badly. The next day she felt dreadful. On Saturday night she was delirious and violently sick. Following a sleepless night, she was violently sick again the next morning and spent most of the day drifting in and out of an uneasy sleep. In the late afternoon Dana finally crawled into a warm bath. The ring on her right hand was hurting and she tried to take it off. It wouldn't budge. Finally, with much soaping and tugging, she managed to remove her ring, leaving her finger swollen and bleeding. Rings are normally circular in shape but this ring had been twisted into a perfect triangle. The ring was made of solid silver and though silver is a malleable metal even the fingers of two strong men could not restore it to its former circle. Finally, a local silversmith with a hammer knocked her ring back into shape. The deep amethyst stone had been partially drained of its colour, leaving it clear and transparent. On that Sunday night Dana had wild nightmares and by Monday morning her watch had stopped working. Dana took it to a jeweller but he said he could do nothing. The watch was completely dead.

Bewitched? Spellbound? Cursed? All the old clichés didn't seem so funny any more, but, hey, this was the twentieth century and stories like that belong to the past. Don't they? Dana felt weak and drained and frightened and she didn't know what to do. She couldn't go to a doctor. She had remembered by then that there is always a grain of truth in folklore, and that being the case, there would be nothing that any doctor could do. She couldn't eat. She could barely take a sip of water. Her legs were unsteady and she felt shaky, light-headed, fragile. Dana kept remembering that mocking laughter. For three days she had been like this. Three days and three nights. A folk memory stirred faintly somewhere. Wasn't three a mystical and magical number to those of all faiths and none? The old pagan cycles of life, death and rebirth. The sky father, the earth mother and the human child of classical belief. The Father, the Son and the Holy Ghost of Christianity.

Suddenly it was gone. Just like that. Whatever it was. For the first time in three days and three nights, Dana felt like herself again.

A tableau of faeries at the silversmith's workshop near the airport, where Dana's ring was mended. The author

On Monday evening she managed to eat some supper and on that night she slept deeply and peacefully. On Tuesday morning she awoke refreshed and recovered as though nothing had been wrong. She could almost believe that she had dreamed the whole thing but that didn't explain the ring or her watch; or the anxious enquiries from her family as to whether she was feeling any better now. A touch of midsummer madness caused through sunstroke, someone suggested? That still didn't explain the ring or her watch, and anyway there had been no sun that day. It was hard to believe the changes which had taken place within the last few hours, and she had been right. No doctor could have helped her.

Two months later Dana returned to Le Trepied. She had to admit she wasn't keen but she wanted to prove something to herself and at least this time she had two big blokes for back-up. Not of course that it made any difference to whoever or whatever inhabited Le Trepied. How stupid she was to think that it would. The next morning at work her left wrist began to burn. The same wrist on which she usually wore her watch, only she'd got wise this time. There was an angry red rash covering the skin, full of little blisters. The following day she went to a local pharmacist, who was puzzled, not sure what the rash was at all. It was unusual. That didn't surprise her. Eventually she was given some hydrocortisone cream and large plasters with which to keep the rash covered for three days. The rash disappeared as suddenly as it had come. That didn't surprise her either. Dana was beginning to recognize how Le Trepied works and decided that it was much healthier to keep well clear of the place, whatever Mr Girard said.

A few days later, in chance conversation with an islander about Le Trepied, Dana was told the following story of strange events which took place one hot summer about twenty years before:

I am not a person who is afraid of the dark or think about ghostly or strange or weird goings on; but what happened to me and two of my good friends at that time I will never forget.

I was thirteen, my friends being twelve and fourteen years old. We used to camp out in our back gardens in order to sneak out in the early morning hours and roam about, have a sneaky cigarette, do all the things we shouldn't have been doing. On this particular night, probably in late August or early September, we decided to walk down to the low-water mark on a local beach near Le Trepied. I remember there being a little bit of a moon out that night, so you could see without a torch. As we started to walk back up the beach we heard the sound of a galloping horse in the distance. The noise became louder and louder and appeared to be getting extremely close. We tried to hide behind an outlet pipe on the beach but by now we could hear the horse within feet of us, though we could see nothing. Fear gripped us and my heart was pounding. Instinctively we decided to run for it. Logically we knew we could not outrun a horse but we were terrified. We ran as fast as we could to the nearest shelter, a toilet block, with the sound of the horse's hoofs at our backs. Gasping for breath, we huddled together in a toilet cubicle, scared out of our wits, with the sound of the horse's hoofs stamping around outside ringing in our ears. We stayed that way, not talking or moving a muscle, for about four hours, until the first rays of dawn began to break. Then we crept outside. The horse, or whatever it was, had gone, but I will never forget the feeling of utter terror that engulfed us all that night.

But hey, this was the twentieth century and stories like that belong to the past. Don't they? But there has long been a legend that 'on wild stormy nights a white horse with flames of fire darting from its nostrils galloped three times round the old chapel [of St George]'. The Rue des Delisles runs directly from the old chapel through Kings Mill along the Rue du Dos D'Ane and La Grande Rue to L'Erée, where these events took place. A white horse can represent the ancient Celtic horse goddess, Epona, and there is also an elemental white horse which sometimes roams woodland areas. Ted Hughes, the late Poet Laureate, a deeply spiritual Yorkshireman who knew his mythology, recognized this elemental white horse when he saw it among the trees near his house during the early 1980s and he wrote a haunting poem about it. Closer to home is the folk tale of young Guernsey folk disguising themselves in the skulls and skins of various beasts and parading the islands in procession on the eve of certain festivals. This practice was supposedly banned on the island around 1600, but stocks of horse skulls were kept in houses on Sark for this purpose until at least the nineteenth century. Then there were the 'de damnatis', the bands of human werewolves (see Chapter 7, 'Call of the Werewolf'), who had roamed the island for two hundred years, drinking, raping and pillaging like the Norsemen of a thousand years before.

In prehistoric times Guernsey was revered as a special place of sanctity by early peoples. The number of surviving remnants of an ancient ritual landscape, such as standing stones, stone circles, dolmens, and the two mother goddess menhirs in St Martins and Câstel churchyards suggest that, like the Isles of Scilly off Cornwall, Guernsey and its off-islands may have been regarded as a part of the 'Celtic otherworld', the 'islands far across and sometimes under the Western Ocean'. Like the Scillies, Guernsey is a slowly drowning landscape. Within historic times the Christian Church also recognized that Guernsey had a special sanctity and by the late medieval period there were a dozen churches and as many chapels on the island. An island survey carried out in 1921 shows a greater density of standing stones, stone circles, crosses, chapels and holy wells than today, but much was destroyed during the Occupation years, 1940–45. The pagan Celts, however, are not the people who built Le Trepied and the witches are not the pagan Celts.

What did happen to Dana out at Le Catioroc? Was it just the

results of imagination and superstition? Who or what inhabits Le Trepied? Was there some elemental force out there controlled by unseen powers? Was the power of generations of witches held in those stones? Was this the witches' revenge for the treatment and torture meted out to them (see Chapter 13, 'Bewitching Guernsey')? Was that why Guernsey folk have been so scared of witchcraft down the centuries? The Priaulx Library on Guernsey holds two ancient books which were kept hidden for centuries on the island. They are known as *Le Grand Albert* and *Le Petit Albert* and they are said to be the works of the Devil himself. Were they the secret books of 'de damnatis'? No one really knows. No one is really inclined to find out. There is still much superstition on Guernsey and perhaps with good reason. There are some things that it seems just cannot be explained.

Was there a natural explanation for what happened to Dana? Science has discovered that some types of granite give off a strong magnetism, strong enough to interfere with electricity supplies, and it is not unreasonable to suppose that this could have an adverse effect on those of a certain chemical make-up. Reason says that this is the most acceptable explanation, followed perhaps by a touch of superstitious imagination, but could that explain what happened to Dana's ring or her watch? Romance says that she disturbed some ancient source of energy and power held in the stones of that ritual landscape built by our forefathers in the old golden land of long ago – but hey, this is the twenty-first century and stories like that belong to the past. Don't they?

CHAPTER 18

The Magic of Brown & Polson

1914

'. . . packets of powder buried about two feet deep . . . at cardinal points of the compass.'

Is there magic in a simple blancmange powder? The question is more suitable as the subject of a spoof and probably none too sober undergraduate debate, than as a serious matter for the police and the Royal Court of Guernsey which resulted in a successful prosecution for practising witchcraft and the maximum prison sentence then available for such a 'crime'. Amazingly, the last trial for witchcraft on the island took place in just 1914, and centred around the question, 'Is there really magic in blancmange powder?'

Early on the morning of 16 January 1914, PC Adams was called out to the Harbourmaster's office in St Sampson on the island of Guernsey. A local lady named Mrs Houtin had banged on the doors of the office 'in an agitated state', demanding police protection and sobbing with terror because 'a spell of witchcraft had been put on her' for non-payment of a £3 debt and unless she paid immediately she had less than a week to live. She did not have the money to pay and she was hysterical, so much so that PC Adams feared for her sanity and worried that she might even try to kill herself. Adams knew that Mrs Houtin was a Roman Catholic and he managed to persuade her that she should go and see the local priest, Canon Foran. He could offer little in the way of help, except to suggest that she go home and pray, but he did manage to calm her down sufficiently for PC Adams and PC Lihou to take a statement from her the following day.

The lady, however, was still clearly terrified and when the policemen arrived at her house PC Lihou said that she had refused to open the door to them at first. When she did finally let them into the house she said she was 'being driven mad by the evil eye'. She had gone to St Peter Port police station in the early hours of the previous morning pleading for help but they had simply

The Harbourmaster's office in St Sampson where a hysterical Mrs Houtin, sobbing with terror, sought help. The author

sent her back to St Sampson, which was why she had been banging desperately on the door of the Harbourmaster's office at half past six in the morning. To calm her down, PC Lihou conducted a preliminary search of the premises but all he found was a box of powder in the outhouse and some charms for members of her family. She recoiled in fright at the sight of his discoveries and said that she 'was afraid to touch the box of powder and thought it was full of little devils'.

Mrs Houtin kept a farm at Croute Fallaize in St Martins. The previous summer her husband had died unexpectedly and then in October someone, she said, had 'bewitched' her cattle and they all died. She was also suffering from bad headaches and in desperation she had gone for help to a lady named Aimée Lake (née Queripel) who lived at the Robegerie in St Sampson. Aimée Lake made a living for herself and her children by 'reading the cards', telling fortunes, explaining the significance of dreams, and dispensing 'charms' made of harmless everyday ingredients such as flour, starch and baking powder.

Mrs Lake had made some tea for herself and Mrs Houtin and they had chatted companionably. Afterwards Mrs Lake read the tea-leaves in her cup, which told her that Mrs Houtin was under a spell, the same as her late husband, Mr Houtin, had been at the time of his death. Accordingly Mrs Lake gave Mrs Houtin 'some salt to throw at her enemies' and some 'magic' powders. She was to burn some of the powders and bury the remainder in the garden. This she did, but, although the powders had taken away her headaches, she was so ill after carrying out Mrs Lake's

Rue de la Fallaize, St Martin, *c.*1920. The street where Mrs Houtin had her farm. Packets of Brown & Polson's blancmange powder were buried in the farmhouse garden to 'ward off evil spirits'. Reproduced by kind permission of the Priaulx Library, St Peter Port, Guernsey

instructions that, tended by her daughter, Rosine Goubert, Mrs Houtin had spent three days in bed recovering. She had paid Mrs Lake 15 francs in October 1913 for these powders followed by £2 15s. (£2.75) shortly afterwards. Now Mrs Lake was telling her that she had put a spell on her and unless she paid another £3 by Friday 23 January 1914 she would die.

On 20 January 1914 *The Star* reported that Mrs Aimée Lake had been charged by Constable E H Ogier of St Sampson with 'fortune telling, the explanation of dreams, and with practising the art of witchcraft from . . . August 1913 . . . till the present day'. When charged, Aimée Lake fainted. When she recovered she panicked. At first she denied the allegations but when she was shown 'certain charms' she collapsed and begged forgiveness. She would give refunds to everyone. She never charged for fortune-telling, though she would accept donations. She was only trying to help. She had never intended to hurt anyone. She would apologize to everyone. It was not enough. This was not the first complaint to be made against her, and the police intended to take action.

Meanwhile PC Adams and PC Lihou set to work and dug up a number of packets of powder buried about two feet deep in Mrs Houtin's back garden at cardinal points of the compass. The holes for the powders had been dug out by her son, Ernest Louvel, and he had then watched his mother bury them. He believed that they were supposed to drive away witches and the 'evil spirits'. He didn't seem to be sure what the powders contained but he knew and was concerned that his mother was very distressed at the misfortunes that she had suffered and he knew that her headaches pained her greatly. If she was not bewitched in some way or had the 'evil eye' laid upon her, then what was causing her problems?

Other witnesses came forward. One of Mrs Lake's employees claimed that she had seen her mistress telling fortunes with cards. Marie Roger said she had paid Mrs Lake £3 10s. for some advice and was given a ring to keep spells off her while she was in Alderney. Felicité Garnier, a child of ten, who lived with Marie Roger, said she had seen Mrs Lake burning powders. Joseph Orphelin had paid £7 10s. plus a further £3 10s. to Mrs Lake for such powders and another £4 for threepenny charms, which were little red bags of imitation pearls and a small bag of ground glass. He then paid yet another £4 for powders and his wife paid a further £2 for advice after being told by Mrs Lake that a spell had been cast over their family.

The saying that a fool and his money are soon parted springs to mind, but one has to view this whole matter in context. The belief in witchcraft was still so strong at this time that it was even considered unlucky not have witch ledges built into the chimney stack of a house where passing witches could rest on their travels, flight by broomstick presumably being less comfortable than by more conventional forms of air travel. The best-known example of a witch ledge can be seen at the Longfrie Hotel in St Pierre du Bois and sports a life-size witch tastefully clad in a ragged black dress and a pointed hat. Mrs Lake had also told Orphelin that she was connected with special societies for science and research in Paris and Belgium and that she sent there for her 'special powders'. Guernsey on the eve of the Great War was an isolated, superstitious community which fervently believed in witches, werewolves, fairies and magic. The 'power' of 'witch charms' depends more on the beliefs of those using them than on anything else and similar 'charms' can still be found on sale in various 'New Age' shops today. The writer of this book reflected wryly that the kindly St Peter Port pharmacist who made up a bottle of rose

Belief in witchcraft is still strong in Guernsey. Witch resting on a chimney ledge at the Longfrie Inn, St Pierre du Bois. The author

water for her to use in baking cakes and biscuits could well have found himself facing a charge of 'witchcraft' had he lived in the early years of the twentieth century; for no other reason than his skill in mixing simple elements to make a new product, which would have been seen as some form of magic in Aimée Lake's day.

When Aimée Lake came to trial she defended herself by saying that people came to her of their own free will and asked her for help. She denied that she was a witch and said that she simply tried to help those with problems by the use of her special powders. However, by this time the powders had been analyzed. They contained baking powder and brown starch plus copious amounts of Brown & Polson's cornflour, from which blancmange is made. Another of her employees, Emily Radstone, said that she regularly bought quantities of ground rice and Brown & Polson's cornflour for Mrs Lake. This rather destroyed the credibility of her claims that the powders came from Paris, but boiled down to the simple question, 'Could there really be magic in blancmange powder?'

It appears that the Guernsey Royal Court seriously thought that there could. Quite possibly influenced by the fact that one of Mrs Lake's ancestors, Alechette Queripel, had been burned at the stake as a witch in 1598, the court found Aimée Lake guilty of witchcraft and sentenced her to eight days' imprisonment. Mrs Lake protested her innocence vehemently and, her husband being in

Canada, asked what would become of her 'fatherless little children' if she were sent to prison. The Sheriff told her not to worry and said that he would take care of them until her release. He seemed determined that she should go to prison for practising her witchcraft. HM Comptroller sensibly said that Mrs Houtin had suffered natural misfortunes and that Mrs Lake had gone too far in demanding money with menaces from stupid and gullible people. The Royal Court then spoiled this by regretting that eight days was the maximum possible sentence for witchcraft, and that a heavier penalty could not be inflicted, before requesting HM Procureur to ask for an increase in the prison term for all future crimes of witchcraft. This might well have happened had it not been for the advent of the Great War, after which life was never quite the same again.

Overlooking the more serious crime of demanding money with menaces, the Royal Court was, amazingly, concerned that a few small bags of blancmange powder 'full of little devils' had been buried in someone's garden at 'cardinal points of the compass'. HM Comptroller had summed up the situation correctly. Mrs Houtin had lost her husband suddenly and this was followed by the natural misfortune of her cows sickening and dying. She was grieving and worried. Her fierce headaches were probably migraines brought on by stress. However, the Royal Court ignored this sensible and likely explanation, preferring to jail Mrs Lake for witchcraft instead. Had the Court's request to HM Procureur succeeded, all those who mixed anything with blancmange powder would be at risk

Brown & Polson's cornflour which Mrs Lake gave wrapped in little bags to Mrs Houtin to bury in her garden. The author

Aimée and John Lake with Henrietta at the back, Florence and Walter David on his mother's lap.

of breaking the law and landing themselves in jail. However, the war broke out soon after this case and somehow the legislation on sentencing for convictions on charges of witchcraft never was changed. Though the world has finally moved on in Guernsey, it is hard not to smile when faced with the neatly stacked shelves of Brown & Polson's cornflour in island supermarkets. The whole story is an ad-man's dream.

Chapter 19

A Christmas Murder

1899

'. . . he . . . "literally smashed her face and head to pieces" . . .'

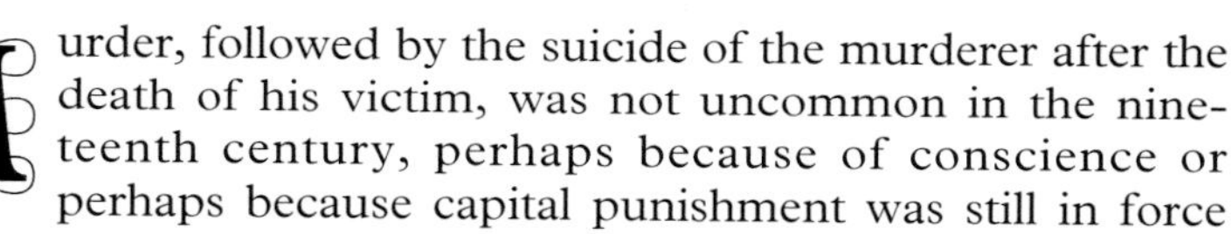

Murder, followed by the suicide of the murderer after the death of his victim, was not uncommon in the nineteenth century, perhaps because of conscience or perhaps because capital punishment was still in force and the murderer knew that he would 'swing for his crime' eventually anyway. Often this left a lot of questions unanswered – principally the reason why the murder had been committed in the first place. Sometimes a motive was obvious; in other cases it was not, and when the murderer was already dead there was little chance of ever establishing the reason why.

Madame Henriette Mouton was a Frenchwoman who was sixty-seven years old at the time of this story. She lived near Beaulieu on Vale Road in St Sampson and kept a lodging house for single men, which provided her with a decent enough living. Although everyone spoke French on the island, she preferred the company of her own countrymen and in 1899 she had three Frenchmen renting rooms from her. One of them was Monsieur Theophile Buret, a thirty-six-year-old quarryman who worked on the island. At that time there were 268 quarries on the island, of which half were in Vale Parish and forty-two were in St Sampson.

Madame Mouton's house was in quite a pleasant part of St Sampson and she took pride in it. She had placed a small Christmas tree in the front parlour, one of the better innovations of the late Prince Consort, she thought. She wondered if Queen Victoria had ever stopped grieving for Prince Albert. Widowhood could be lonely. That was another benefit of taking in lodgers. They were company of a sort and they all had one thing in common. Like the great French writer, Victor Hugo, who had lived on Guernsey for fifteen years, they all missed their homeland.

Two days before Christmas 1899, Saturday 23 December, the

household was up early as usual. Madame Mouton always made breakfast for herself and her lodgers. She ate her own breakfast with them round the kitchen table. It was a chance to talk and exchange news. The other two left for work at 6.30 am, leaving Madame Mouton and Buret still eating breakfast together. Madame Mouton obviously had no qualms about being on her own with Monsieur Buret. Conversation was muted. Madame Mouton had Christmas to think about. Exactly what happened will never be known, but some disagreement must have ensued, although there is no record of any dispute or dissension between the two of them. Whatever it was could hardly have justified what happened next.

In what must have been 'the heat of the moment' during the quarrel, for it is practically inconceivable that Buret would have planned such an attack to take place in the middle of breakfast, he suddenly snapped and, seizing a chopper lying nearby, 'literally smashed her face and head to pieces', after which he 'slashed what was left of her face with a bread knife'. He had hit her so hard that 'pieces of her flesh were left sticking to the chopper'. By the time he came to his senses, Madame Mouton lay in a dreadful bloodied heap at his feet. The whole kitchen was covered in blood and so was Buret. This was a truly strange and macabre murder, yet no one seems to have heard anything. It is unlikely that the first blow killed Madame Mouton and Buret hit her in the face so she must have seen him coming. Yet there were no screams, no sounds of a struggle or of any desperate attempts to escape. The force he used on her must have required some effort and if his motive was hatred of her for some unknown reason, at the very least it might be expected that he would raise his voice, shout something, even grunt. Eerily, it appears as though this terrible killing took place in virtual silence.

Buret made no attempt to cover up his crime. Dazed and shocked though he must have been, he obviously changed his clothes, for he went out shortly afterwards and no one remarked upon his appearance. He took the tram into St Peter Port. He was calm enough but he seems to have appeared to be somewhat distracted. Buret went straight to Madame Hauzé's house in Fountain Street, from where he withdrew £13. This might be thought an odd thing to do and an odd amount to withdraw, but people often saved for their own or family funerals through burial clubs and it offers the most likely explanation for why Buret should do such a thing. The horror of what he had done had hit him and he had already planned his course of action. Catching the tram back to St Sampson, Buret returned straightaway to the 'bloodbath

St Peter Port, *c.*1904. Author's collection

house'. He went upstairs to his room and fetched his razor. Then he lay down beside the body of Madame Mouton with its shattered face and cut his throat. Shortly afterwards a neighbour called to wish Madame Mouton the greetings of the season. Getting no reply, she tapped on the back door and, calling out to Madame Mouton, she went in. Her screams raised the alarm.

Someone called the doctor and someone called the police. Dr Leale examined the couple, she lying on her back and he on his face in the blood-soaked kitchen. Madame Mouton was, of course, quite dead. Her remains were placed in a coffin and removed to the mortuary in the Harbourmaster's office at St Sampson. Buret was barely alive. He had lost a lot of blood but the doctor stitched his wound and ordered him to be taken to the Town Hospital. However, Buret was by now very weak and the three-inch wound on the left-hand side of his throat was still bleeding badly. The party stopped at the Harbourmaster's office so that Buret could rest but it was too late. Here, lying just a few yards from the woman he had so savagely butchered, Theophile Buret died, and with him the reasons for committing such an horrific act of violence.

The local community was shocked. They were not used to such bloody murder. Drunken squabbles and accidental death during a fight were more the norm. There was little need for a post mortem and the inquest was a formality. Buret, as a suicide, could not be buried in consecrated ground but had to lie outside the churchyard walls. The Christmas bells pealed out over Guernsey, ringing the good tidings of the season and calling the church congregations to go and offer thanks for their Saviour's birth; but that year the normal yuletide greeting of 'peace and goodwill to all men' rang a little hollow in the ears of St Sampson residents. The last Christmas of the old century had been one that none of them would ever forget.

CHAPTER 20

A Brecqhou Wrecking

1781

'. . . it was the only chance most of them would ever have to own something so rich and beautiful.'

Today Brecqhou is a private island owned by the reclusive Barclay brothers, who are the proprietors of the *Daily Telegraph*. Security is strict and all that can really be seen of the island is the somewhat incongruous 'pink fairytale palace' built by the brothers in the 1990s which stands close to the summit of the small island. It is to the Reverend Cachemaille, vicar of Sark during the latter part of the nineteenth century, that history is indebted for a glimpse of Brecqhou, though his description of life on the island then gives a completely different picture from modern times: 'there is . . . a little harbour on the west with a good road leading from it . . . there are neither trees nor shrubs upon the island . . . the summit is an . . . extended plain, which for centuries was left uncultivated . . . it was anciently kept as a rabbit warren . . . a few sheep were sometimes left there.'

Cachemaille goes on to explain that around 1830 a house was built as two cottages and rented to a couple of families from Sark. However, due to constant bickering this was reduced to 'a single family only, whose members may comfort each other in the full sense of the complete independence they enjoy – no poor rates, no taxation, no militia service . . . no school, nor church . . . sometimes during the prevalence of prolonged gales, the inhabitants of Brecqhou have been reduced to extremities, without bread, flour, or other necessaries of life'. He adds that around the cottage 'the wild abandon of the whole surroundings suggest innumerable subjects for the painter . . . but truth obliges us to confess that . . . some attention to sanitary improvement is here urgently called for'. Despite this, the 'picturesque' little house of La Frégondée, with its 'composite pigstye' found its few moments of fame in the nineteenth-century novel *The Doctor's*

Dilemma by Hesba Stretton as a place of refuge which she renamed Tardif's Cottage.

About fifty years beforehand, in the autumn of 1781, the romantically named *Valentine*, a ship belonging to the East India Company, became separated in a strong south-westerly gale from the fleet being escorted by the frigate *Apollo*. The ship anchored near Nesté, a rock on the north-east point of Brecqhou. The captain, however, 'commanded a little more chain to be paid out, so as to ease anchors', and the *Valentine* promptly struck on the rocky bottom. He was an experienced man and there was some surprise expressed that he had decided on this course of action. There were rumours that he was maliciously advised by a local pilot or sailor who knew very well what would be likely to happen. However, the vessel was fatally holed and sank rapidly, though the crew managed to scramble to safety on the then desolate and uninhabited island of Brecqhou.

The East India Company was probably the first 'multinational' and they had grown rich on the proceeds. Despite the name, the

Brecqhou and Guillot Passage *c.*1910. The scene of the wrecking of the East India Company ship *Valentine*. Reproduced by kind permission of the Priaulx Library, St Peter Port, Guernsey

company traded between India, Africa and Europe. The *Valentine* was laden with cotton, silks and gold dust. Indian silks and cottons were much prized for their beautiful colours, the feel of the material and its durability. There was great demand in England for these wares and they would fetch a good price. The Industrial Revolution, which would bring such luxuries within the reach of ordinary working people, was still in its infancy.

When the *Valentine* broke up, her cargo was dispersed in the waves. The escorting frigate was tacking up and down trying to find the missing ship, her cargo and her crew, while the Sarkese watched the proceedings from their high vantage points on the steep cliffs of Sark. As soon as the wind abated a little, the Sark boats put out to sea to rescue the floating bales and strong boxes. This was the age of the privateers, and ships of the East India Company would have been regarded as fair game. Someone somewhere would have argued that the cargo was meant to help an enemy of the British Crown and that therefore it was completely justifiable to keep it. Soldiers from Guernsey were at once dispatched to camp out on Brecqhou to guard what was salvaged and prevent pillaging, but it was a forlorn hope that much salvage would be declared. Some of the Sarkese brought what they found to Brecqhou and deposited the goods with the soldiers. Some brought a proportion. Many did not, however, and in Cachemaille's time 'some houses still preserve . . . rich and magnificent silken brocades derived from this shipwreck'.

Although the Indian cottons and silks would have been worth a great deal of money the Sarkese preferred, or so it seemed, to keep their newly acquired material treasure for themselves. Perhaps after all it was the only chance most of them would ever have to own something so rich and beautiful. It is not recorded if the soldiers stationed on Brecqhou made any attempt to retrieve the items that made their way to Sark, but they would have been ill-advised to do so because Sark has its own medieval feudal laws and, even if they could have landed on the island in the stormy weather, they would have been wrong-footed from the start. Better, they decided, to hand over to the authorities what they had been given and allow them to believe that the rest had been lost at sea. The ordinary Sarkese were not the only ones to benefit from this unexpected wreck. The Seigneur retrieved two iron cannons from the ship which he had mounted near the watch-house on the Eperquerie. Pieces of Indian dyewood also floated ashore and in time much of the iron ballast which the ship had carried was also retrieved by the islanders. Laws of salvage, such as there were, tended to be ignored and it was often a case of 'finders keepers'. Wrecks, after all, were 'a gift from the sea'.

This episode is one of the few recorded pieces of history that exists for Brecqhou. It is also, to date, the island's only recorded instance of crime or 'foul deed'.

Chapter 21

How Did She Die?

1899

'. . . when they returned Françoise was lying on the foot of the bed crying "My head! My head!"'

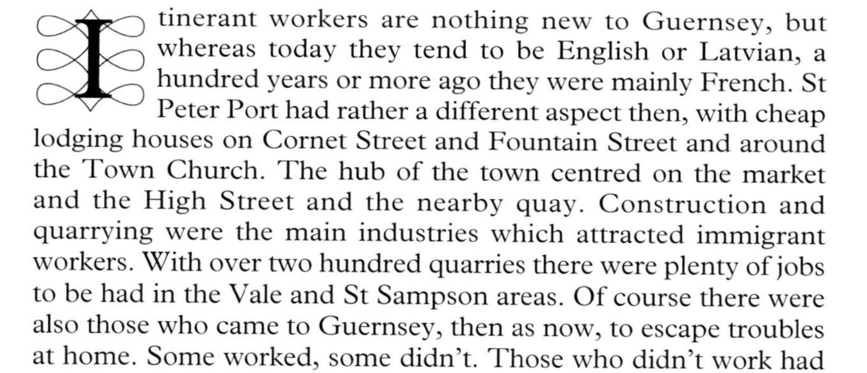

Itinerant workers are nothing new to Guernsey, but whereas today they tend to be English or Latvian, a hundred years or more ago they were mainly French. St Peter Port had rather a different aspect then, with cheap lodging houses on Cornet Street and Fountain Street and around the Town Church. The hub of the town centred on the market and the High Street and the nearby quay. Construction and quarrying were the main industries which attracted immigrant workers. With over two hundred quarries there were plenty of jobs to be had in the Vale and St Sampson areas. Of course there were also those who came to Guernsey, then as now, to escape troubles at home. Some worked, some didn't. Those who didn't work had more time for drinking and mischief.

René Victor Trouvé was a Frenchman from Banis, Île et Vilaine, and he lived in a room of a lodging house on Cornet Street in St Peter Port with fellow Frenchman Pierre Marie Gorel and a lady named Françoise Marie Conan. The room had a double bed and there was a divan against one wall. There was a rough wooden table under the window with two or three upright wooden chairs set round it. A wardrobe stood in one corner and a dresser in another next to a rickety old kitchen stove. It was cramped for three people to share and there was precious little privacy. Françoise's sister, Jeanne, also had a room in the house and it was likely that the two sisters had shared until Françoise met Trouvé. While some families in Guernsey were very rich, there were also a large number of poor folk who were forced to live in similar conditions. Tempers flared quickly and alcohol offered one of the few means of escape from such circumstances.

French was still the official language in Guernsey so Trouvé would have had no difficulty in making himself understood or in finding work. However, times were hard and both René and Françoise drank, sometimes to excess. There was little else to do. Often there were rows. It seemed a hopeless existence. At weekends it was worse. On the Saturday night of 28 January 1899 they had a violent quarrel and around midnight to one o'clock Françoise was heard shouting and making a terrible noise by her neighbours, Mrs Sourcoupe and Mrs Queripel. Fights were commonplace in such lodging houses, especially when drink was involved, and at the time no one gave it much thought. This fight proved to be different, however, for two weeks later Françoise Conan was dead.

An inquest was held shortly after her death which had taken place on Saturday 11 February. Françoise had received a wound to her head and it appeared that her death might not be due to natural causes. The wound was said to have been caused by a fall she'd had on Saturday 28 January. Françoise had later gone to a doctor for medical treatment and received a prescription which she had obtained from Mr Carré, a chemist on The Bordage in St Peter Port. However, Mrs Caroline Carré, who lived opposite Françoise in Cornet Street, had heard her screaming, in both pain and anger, until one o'clock on Sunday morning 29 January. This corroborated the evidence of Françoise's neighbours. Then René and Françoise's room-mate, Pierre Marie Gorel, told a story that seemed to suggest that Françoise had not fallen but that she had been attacked. According to Gorel, Françoise had been drunk the day before, and in the evening of the day of the quarrel Trouvé had pushed her down. He must have been violent towards her for Gorel had actually gone to fetch the police and when they returned Françoise was lying on the foot of the bed crying 'My head! My head!'

An indictment for a fatal assault, which should really have been a murder charge, was issued against René Trouvé and the trial began on Tuesday 21 March at the Royal Court. He pleaded not guilty to fatally assaulting Françoise Conan. Jeanne Conan, Françoise's sister, told the court that she had not heard any quarrel and on the Monday had noticed nothing wrong with her sister, but on the Tuesday morning Trouvé had sent for her because Françoise was ill. Françoise had then told her that she had been assaulted by Trouvé and that he'd kicked her. Jeanne went to get some medicine for her sister but when she brought it back, Trouvé refused to let her in to their room. Jeanne then immediately went to fetch PC Ward, who found the door of the room open when he arrived. The following week, she said, Françoise had complained of further pains in her head. Jeanne had tried to

Upper Cornet Street, St Peter Port, where René Trouvé lived with Françoise Conan. Reproduced by kind permission of the Priaulx Library, St Peter Port, Guernsey

care for her and help her but Françoise had died on the following Saturday.

PC Ward, uneasy about the situation altogether, had returned to Françoise's room on the Wednesday, the day after Jeannne had called him out. Trouvé and Gorel were eating a meal at the table and Françoise was lying on the bed. Trouvé said that Françoise had a head wound from falling down some steps and Françoise, who seemed to be in some kind of 'stupefied state', had agreed. On the Thursday Marie Prijent said that she had seen Françoise and that she seemed to be ill and that she had complained of pains in her head. After Françoise died on the Saturday, PC Ward had sent for Dr Gibson because he was not at all satisfied that this death was a natural death.

Dr Gibson and Dr Collenette performed an autopsy, which showed that Françoise's death had been caused through blows to the head. Gorel, however, having at first gone to fetch the police after seeing Trouvé push Françoise, now said that he had been in the room all night and that no blows had been struck. For the defence, Dr Kinnersley said that actual death could have been due to apoplexy and Dr Allen said that no bruises were visible. Jurat Brouard objected volubly to the defence advocate, Victor Carey, calling expert testimony for the defence, but Jurat Ozanne and the Bailiff saw no problem, so the defence doctors' testimony was allowed to stand. No one had seen any blows struck, but several people had heard dreadful cries and screams.

The legal system of Guernsey differs from that of the UK and a jury is composed of Jurats, not the 'twelve good men and true' randomly selected from the general public in England. A Jurat is an elected officer by a body known as the States of Election and he has a number of regular civic responsibilities and duties. After due deliberations HM Procureur and the Controller agreed that death was due to assault, but unfortunately the Jurat vote was split. Jurat Collings, believing that the assault was not premeditated, said that five years' penal servitude would be sufficient punishment. Jurats de Havilland, Carey, McCulloch, and Ozanne wanted twelve years' penal servitude as the sentence, while Jurats Tardif, Le Roy, Le Cocq, de Garis and Brouard demanded twenty years. It was therefore left to the Bailiff to cast the deciding vote and as a result René Trouvé was sentenced to twenty years' penal servitude for a vicious and ultimately fatal assault on Françoise Conan. Life, especially female life, was held cheap in the nineteenth century but the Jurats' eminently sensible verdict meant that justice of a kind was seen to be done for at least one tragic young woman whose life was snuffed out because her man had lost his temper.

Chapter 22

Ghost of the Murdered

1651

'He stabbed at his opponent again and again and within minutes the soldier lay dead.'

Some people believe in ghosts and some don't, since their existence is still 'not proven beyond all possible doubt'. Guernsey folk believed in ghosts, of course. The island abounded with them. Human ghosts. Animal ghosts. Spectral ghosts. Ghosts acting as policemen in the days before there was even a police force, however, was something new, though there is actually a case recorded in the *Calendar of State Papers for England* (1654) where the ghost of a man solved his own murder on the Channel Island of Guernsey. Perhaps it could just be called conscience but then again, perhaps not.

St Peter Port was a thriving port in the seventeenth century and, finally, mostly secure from attacks by the French. The seafront looked different from today. The modern road along the quay did not exist and at high tide the water came right up to the High Street, lapping up the ginnels and former Cow Lane which ran from the quay up the side of the present Le Lievre's kitchen shop to the High Street. Houses clustered around the Town Church and there was still living memory of the burning of witches at the foot of Tower Hill.

In 1651 the *John*, a privateer (see Chapter 10, 'Daylight Robbery') from the Isle of Wight, under Captain John Shapman, put into Guernsey for repairs, refitting and plenty of liquid refreshments. Two of the crew, John Baldock and William Gibson, had become good mates on the last voyage and were looking forward to going ashore and spending their share of the proceeds from the sale of the latest cargo their ship had captured. Gibson had family in Cornwall but he wasn't yet ready to return to them. It is not recorded if or where John Baldock had anyone to call his own.

St Peter Port was full of ale houses and pretty women experienced and adept at tempting unwary sailors and it wasn't long before Baldock and Gibson were extremely drunk. They staggered from pub to pub, arm-in-arm for support, singing, laughing and shouting. As they lurched together through the Town, ever more careless and inebriated, the pair of them cannoned into an English soldier who was almost equally drunk. The soldier staggered and looked at them. He poked Gibson in the chest with his forefinger and told him to get out of the way like a good boy. Gibson pushed the soldier's arm angrily away and swore at him. Who the hell did he think he was anyway? The two men squared up to each other. A fight was inevitable.

It started as a fist fight but it quickly became apparent that Gibson was getting the worst of it. Determined that he was not going to be beaten and humiliated, Gibson drew a knife. He stabbed at his opponent again and again and within minutes the English soldier lay dead. Baldock stared in horror. Gibson was very drunk and he tried to make light of it when he saw the look on Baldock's face, the expression on his own face veering between concern and irritation. He felt no particular guilt. After all, the English soldier had started the fight. Finally Baldock shrugged his shoulders. Gibson was his friend so, although he had not actually committed the deed, he showed his support for it by 'washing his hands in the victim's blood'. He and Gibson robbed the English soldier of 3s. 6d. (worth around £10 sterling at today's values) before he helped Gibson to dump the soldier's body in a nearby ditch. Shortly afterwards William Gibson returned to his home town of Fowey in Cornwall, leaving Baldock on his own in St Peter Port.

What should have been an enjoyable shore leave rapidly turned into the worst kind of nightmare for John Baldock. The English soldier's body had quickly been discovered and a verdict of murder by person or persons unknown had been delivered by the Court. The dead soldier was then decently buried, but not for Baldock. He couldn't stop thinking about what had happened. He tried to drown reality and to blot out his memories by drinking but it didn't work. All he could see was the beaten and bloodied body of the English soldier. Late one night he staggered out of an ale house and morosely started to weave his way home when he became conscious of someone standing in front of him. He looked up and there was a shadowy figure on the pavement. Baldock rubbed his eyes, trying to see the figure more clearly but it seemed to be hovering in a sort of mist. Grumbling, he moved to one side to let it pass when suddenly he came to an abrupt halt. The English soldier was standing there on the street pointing at him. Baldock screamed. He looked wildly around to see if anyone else

Fountain Street, St Peter Port (1799, by Dupuy). One of the streets where John Baldock was haunted by the ghost of the murdered English soldier. Reproduced by kind permission of the Priaulx Library, St Peter Port, Guernsey

was about and when he turned back the apparition had vanished.

The next night the same thing happened again. Baldock was now terrified, both of the apparition and that someone else would see it and would know the truth of the soldier's death; at the same time he wanted someone else to see it just so that he could reassure himself that he was not going mad. The next night was the same, and the next. Baldock was seriously frightened. He changed his habits, his lodgings, the places he drank. He even started going to church. Nothing worked. Everywhere he went the unknown soldier's ghost seemed to materialize, standing just ahead of him or walking behind him, staring, imploring, pointing, haunting Baldock in the streets and alehouses of the Town, in his bed, in his mind and in his dreams.

John Baldock became both hunted and haunted. He sent a message to Gibson imploring him to help; but nothing happened. His ship was not yet due to sail and Baldock had the feeling that even when it did there would be one extra on board. A ghostly stowaway. Everyone else had forgotten the English soldier. The irony was that Baldock and Gibson had committed the perfect crime. No one knew of their involvement except for Baldock and the ghost, but the ghost seemed determined that his death would be properly avenged. He would haunt Baldock to his dying day unless he publicly admitted what he and Gibson had done. He did not dare to talk to anyone about his experiences but he desperately needed to confide in someone. He had not heard from Gibson and he had given up trying to contact him. Either Gibson had moved on from Fowey or he no longer wanted to know Baldock. Either way, the end result was the same. Baldock was on his own. Every night was the same now. Wherever he went the ghost was there. Pointing, accusing, telling him to give himself up.

At last John Baldock could stand it no longer. All he wanted was to confess his guilt and for the thing to leave him alone. Anything would be better than this phantom shadowing his life. Finally, in desperation, Baldock went to the authorities and confessed his crime. He was put into jail while a search was made for Gibson. He had no way of knowing that the story he had told the authorities was so unusual that it would find its way into the sovereign's *Calendar of State Papers for England.* Though Baldock knew that the outcome of what he had done was likely to result in his own death and that of Gibson, he didn't care because at long last the soldier's ghost was quiet. The unquiet spirit had been avenged and John Baldock had finally found a kind of peace.

Chapter 23

The Bailiff's Cross

1320

'Fool! Did I not tell thee not to touch that *rick?'*

In later medieval times Guernsey wasn't a bad place to live, despite the constant attacks by the French since King John had lost Normandy in 1204. Castle Cornet, built in that same year, had done much for the general security of the island, supported by Vale Castle and Château Marais in St Sampson. The priories at the Church of St Michel in Vale and on the tiny island of Lihou offered spiritual guidance along with the dozen or so small chapels built throughout the island. Farming and fishing offered the peasantry a good level of subsistence, and wine from France, as well as from vines grown on the island, was plentiful. Small windmills ground the corn, with some going to the miller and some to the local Seigneur of the particular fief in which the mill was situated. Fresh water was plentiful and there were a number of holy wells dotted about the island. Guernsey was a pretty if remote island and generally folk were contented, but to quote the modern idiom, there is always someone to spoil your day.

According to official records, in 1320 the Bailiff of Guernsey, Walter, or Gautier, de la Salle, was executed for his part in the murder of Ranulph de Gautier. This was the man who, in 1304, had killed the man responsible for the murder of a monk at the Priory on Lihou (see Chapter 27, 'Murders and Mysteries of Lihou'). There is documentary evidence of this in the State records of Edward III (1320–70), for 1323, for de la Salle's wife, Cecilia, 'petitioned for restitution of lands and rentes bought in their name and in that of their children, in the parishes of St Peter Port and St Andrew's; and that these tenements, on account of the death of the said Walter, who was judicially executed last criminal assizes . . . had been seized by the king'. The king was good enough to 'remove his hand' (restore the lands to her). However, three men were responsible for the torture and murder of Ranulph

Gautier, yet de la Salle was the only one to hang. Why was this?

By all accounts Ranulph Gautier had been a deeply unpopular man. There is little doubt that the other two men were de la Salle's accomplices and that de la Salle initiated the whole dreadful process of 'divers torture' by which Gautier met his death in Castle Cornet – but de la Salle was no angel himself. In popular legend it was not just the responsibility for the murder of Gautier which sent him to the gallows, but another plot de la Salle had hatched which would have cost an innocent man his life simply because he would not do exactly as de la Salle wished.

Gautier de la Salle lived on an estate known as La Petite Ville (the little town or village). There has been a manor house on the estate since the thirteenth century, though the house still visible in the nineteenth century dated only to early Tudor times. This was an L-shaped building which had a tower with arrow slits in the angle of the L. The earlier manor house, which was de la Salle's home, pre-dated that building. De la Salle had a poor neighbour named Monsieur Massy. Massy owned a small field at the back of de la Salle's house and he owned an ancient right to draw water from the well in de la Salle's garden. This greatly annoyed Gautier de la Salle and he was determined to put a stop to it. At first he tried to buy off this right and offered Monsieur Massy a reasonably fair price for his field but Monsieur Massy refused to sell: 'The Lord forbid it to me that I should give the inheritance of my fathers to thee', he told de la Salle.

However, de la Salle was determined to be rid of Monsieur Massy, although he had to make it seem legal. He therefore hatched a devious plot. Theft was still then an offence punishable in many cases by the death penalty. It was known that there was ill-feeling between the two men, so de la Salle hid two of his own precious silver cups in a haystack and then contrived, by means of carefully placed circumstantial evidence, to make Monsieur Massy appear to be the culprit responsible for the 'theft' of his cups. Accordingly, Monsieur Massy was accused of theft, taken into custody and imprisoned. De la Salle saw to it that a trial was held. He wanted Monsieur Massy out of the way quickly but he also wanted everything to appear legal and above board. The day of the trial arrived and the carefully created circumstantial evidence was presented. The cups were missing and everything pointed to Monsieur Massy having taken them. Despite his loud protestations of innocence, Monsieur Massy was found guilty of theft and sentenced to death.

On the day of Massy's execution, de la Salle prepared to go to the courthouse and watch an innocent man put to death so that he could buy the field and draw water from his well. Before leaving his house he ordered his servants to remove a particular haystack from the cornfield and store it in the barn. He made his way to the courthouse and saw to his satisfaction the finishing touches being put to the gallows. Soon, he thought, I will not have anything to worry about. He had just taken his seat when one of his servants rushed in and exclaimed loudly, 'The cups are found!' Without thinking, de la Salle leapt to his feet and cried, 'Fool! Did I not tell thee not to touch *that* rick?', before stopping in confusion as he realized what he had said. The execution was halted immediately and Monsieur Massy was declared innocent and given a full pardon.

De la Salle was then put on trial. The hearing was brief, for he had no defence to offer, and he was given the same sentence which he had been prepared to witness Massy suffer. As a convicted felon his estates were confiscated and given to the king. Since that time they have borne the name of La Ville au Roi despite the fact that his wife's lands were restored to her by the king.

As de la Salle was on his way to his execution at Les Galères in St Andrew's he stopped to received the Holy Sacrament at a cross carved into the face of a smooth upright stone, which has given the name Bailiff's Cross (La Croix au Bailiff) to the crossroads near which it stood and to a modern public house at the spot. The stone was in all probability an old standing stone from pagan times which was 'Christianized' by the incision of a cross on one surface. Near the disputed field which ultimately cost de la Salle his life, an old lane, now destroyed by a modern road, on the northern boundary of La Ville au Roi, was called La Rue de l'Ombre de la Mort (the Street of the Shadow of Death) and is reputed to be haunted by a huge headless spectral black dog – and there are those who say that is de la Salle's just and due fate for all eternity.

Chapter 24

Suffer the Little Children

Late 1820s

'So if there had been a baby, what had happened and where was it?'

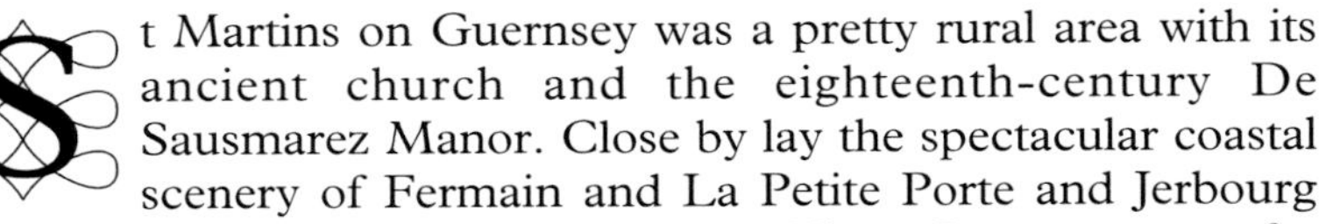

St Martins on Guernsey was a pretty rural area with its ancient church and the eighteenth-century De Sausmarez Manor. Close by lay the spectacular coastal scenery of Fermain and La Petite Porte and Jerbourg Point, and the working harbour of La Vieux Porte was not far away. The place was much more sparsely populated than today and parts of the parish were quite remote. Although St Martins is only a few minutes from St Peter Port now by car or bus, it took a considerable time to travel there in the nineteenth century. The roads were either exceptionally bad or non-existent and a journey to Pleinmont, which takes half an hour today, could take up to two days. During the seventeenth century bands of young men 'went about in werewolfery' on the island, particularly in St Martins, terrorizing the local population and preying on young itinerant female servants whom they would attack as they walked to and from the large houses of the district where they worked. Consequently island girls became nervous of this type of employment and it became much more the custom to have live-in servants. This brought its own problems, in that having young, single and often attractive girls under the same roof proved too much of a temptation for many employers.

Sometime in the late 1820s Sarah Elliott, a young maidservant from Exeter, had come to Guernsey with her brother in search of work. While he obtained employment in the St Sampson/St Peter Port area, Sarah found a live-in position at the house of Monsieur Marie-Joseph François Beasse on the Rouette du Braye in St Martins. For this she was grateful even though it meant living apart from her brother. Sarah liked Guernsey and enjoyed working for Monsieur Beasse, and she often thought how lucky she was to be there, but her happiness was not to last. Before long Sarah found herself pregnant. During the nineteenth century it was a serious and unacceptable social disgrace to have a baby out of wedlock and Sarah was dismayed. She did not dare to tell her brother of her predicament, but she did confide in her employer, who was almost certainly the father of her baby. However, as in England, men of his station in life did not marry girls of her station in life. In order to conceal the pregnancy, it was therefore decided that she should go back to Exeter to have the child and then perhaps have it adopted. So she did not make any preparations for this baby. There was 'no linen provided for him, no clothes for him to wear, no cradle for him to lie in'.

Meanwhile Sarah's brother had not seen her for some time and he was becoming increasingly concerned about her. He walked up to St Martins to see her one fine Sunday afternoon and became seriously alarmed for her when he met an old lady on the road to St Martins who told him that she had been called in to do Sarah's work while Sarah was away visiting her sick brother. However, when he reached the house on the Rouette du Braye he could get no reply. Sarah, as it turned out, had never actually left the island. A week before her intended departure she went into premature labour and on Friday, 11 June 1830 she gave birth to a son at her employer's house. Around this time her brother called once more and asked to see her but he was again refused. When he tried to insist he was thrown off Beasse's property. By now he was seriously worried. The next day he tried to see her yet again and this time he succeeded, and he was shocked. He noticed a great change in her appearance although he did not then know that she had recently given birth. So worried was he that he called in Assistant Constable Hancock because he feared that his sister was being ill-treated and that she was too frightened to admit it.

After the Assistant Constable had made a few enquiries Sarah's brother began to suspect the truth: that she had been pregnant and she had been too scared to tell him. However, if she had been pregnant, where was the baby? What had happened to it? He had seen or heard no sign of a baby in the house when he had paid her a visit. He then called in the Attorney General Delegate because his concern was growing and he was not getting any answers to his questions. The Attorney General wasn't satisfied either and the Royal Court pressed for further investigation. Officers called at the house. Sarah was still confined to bed. What, they asked, was wrong with her? They had good reason to believe that she had been pregnant. It wasn't easy to keep a secret like that in a small tightly knit community like Guernsey. So if there had been a baby, what had happened and where was it?

All this proved too much for Monsieur Beasse and he finally

Poor children of St Peter Port in the late nineteenth century. Reproduced by kind permission of the Priaulx Library, St Peter Port, Guernsey

broke down and confessed. Sarah had gone into labour early and had given birth prematurely. He hadn't called the doctor or midwife beforehand because both he and Sarah had been anxious not to publicize the pregnancy and he thought that Sarah would know what to do when the time came. However, the baby, a little boy, had been stillborn. Sarah was distraught so he had buried the child in the garden because he did not want to cause her further distress. As the baby had been born dead, he had decided to spare Sarah's feelings as much as possible and tried to salvage both their reputations.

Orders were immediately given for the child to be disinterred and a Coroner's Inquest took place on the same day, Monday 14 June, before Bailiff Daniel de Lisle Brock. However, the medical examination results did not support Beasse's story of a stillbirth. Blood found around the baby's mouth indicated foul play. Further medical witnesses were called. Then the Bailiff ordered that the tiny unnamed baby should be interred in consecrated ground. He was placed in a small coffin and buried, unmourned and unloved by those who should have cared for him. The following day, Tuesday 15 June, Beasse was further examined. Finally his confession and the medical details statement were made before De Lisle Brock and two Jurats on 16 June.

The statement, which indicted both Beasse and Sarah, does not make for comfortable reading:

> *being accused of either alone, or with [his/her] accomplices, in the night of the 10th or 11th June, 1830, or thereabouts, within, or near to a house belonging to Mr Marie-Joseph Beasse, situated at the Rouette du Braye in the parish of St Martins, having introduced an instrument into the throat and also the anus of the said child, in such a manner as to cause the death of the said child, and which child was secretly buried in a garden behind the said house belonging to the said Beasse; also for having the said Elliott, or accomplices, concealed and denied her pregnancy and delivery, not having given the said infant the necessary succors and assistance at the time of its birth; and not having called a midwife or other person at the time of her delivery . . .*

Sarah Elliott, however, was still confined to bed because she had been delivered of a baby without medical help. Afterwards there had been a lot of blood and Beasse had called the doctor for her. Dr Mauger had attended her and had seen the body of the infant lying on the table, but stillbirths or death shortly after birth were common then. One might have expected him to have been at least curious but he said he had had no reason at that stage to be suspicious or to examine the baby. Given the state of Sarah and results of the post mortem he must have felt the need to cover his back.

Beasse had retained Advocate Jeremie to act for him and Sarah retained Advocate Falla. Both Sarah and Beasse pleaded not guilty but both of them were indicted and sent for trial. The Court could hardly do otherwise in the light of the post mortem results. Despite her condition, Sarah was ordered to attend court on 17 June, where she appeared to be much distressed throughout the proceedings. She sobbed as she was questioned and broke down when the Court announced its verdict. She got little sympathy for she was an unmarried mother, a non-islander, and a possible child murderess. In spite of everything it seems likely that Beasse really did care for Sarah since he tried, however clumsily, to help her and he paid for her medical care and her legal representation. Sarah had intended to return to Guernsey after the birth, which indicates that a relationship existed between her and Beasse.

The baby's death may well have been the result of pure panic, since Sarah had obviously not intended to kill her child if she had arranged to go to Exeter, her home town, to give birth, where the baby might be discreetly adopted. It would also explain why she had made no provision on Guernsey for her baby. It is most likely that Beasse actually killed the baby since Sarah would not have been in any state to do this immediately after the birth. She was exhausted, bleeding heavily, and it would have gone against all her natural instincts. Sarah and Beasse stuck to their stories and supported each other throughout. Although the outcome was tragically clear, the real truth of exactly what took place between Sarah Elliott and Marie-Joseph Beasse that summer day in 1830 is a secret which both of them took to their graves.

CHAPTER 25

The Island of Death

Early 1940s

'. . . a fantastic picture presented itself . . . there were skeletons all over the place . . .'

Alderney is the most northerly and least sheltered of the four larger Channel Islands (Jersey, Guernsey, Sark and Alderney), the closest to France, and the only one of the Islands to almost be completely evacuated during the Second World War (11 out of 1,800 remained). Alderney is not a large island, measuring about 5 kilometres in length by 2 kilometres wide. The wind howls for much of the time, seemingly coming from all directions, and the island has a remote, otherworldly air about it. Although fairly mild in summer, it can be bitterly cold in winter and the wind-chill factor makes it far worse. The town of St Anne would hardly rate as a town on the English mainland, more a large village, but it has a good museum, a bookshop and a library, a pottery, a number of very decent places to eat as much as one can, three of the 'Big Four' banks (Barclays are absent) and a charity shop called The Stock Exchange. The Church of St Anne is dedicated to St Anne, mother of the Virgin Mary, and is known as the Cathedral of the Channel Islands. Most of the architecture is built of grey stone, which combines with the rocky terrain to give the island a very grey aspect. The railway, built by slave workers during the German Occupation (1940–45), runs from Braye Harbour to Mannez Quarry, but there is little railway romance in the small shunting engine which pulls two carriages acquired from the Metropolitan Line of the London Underground up to the quarry. Here the rusty trucks and what looks suspiciously like a Heath Robinson combine harvester, abandoned under the grim concrete German lookout tower, make it seem as if the Germans left only yesterday.

A grey island under a grey sky surrounded by a grey sea. Alderney hides so many grim secrets of foul deeds, of suspicious deaths, of outright murder. Stories of what happened remain

German underground fortifications on Alderney, Second World War, built by slave labourers. The author

untold or unfinished because a veil has been drawn across Alderney's history during those five years of war. Thanks to the destruction of German war records by the Nazis, the disappearance of Alderney's archives during the Occupation, and the withholding of vital information on wartime Alderney by the British Government for 100 years (until 2045), the early 1940s have proved to be Alderney's own Dark Ages, in more ways than one.

The island forms part of the Bailiwick of Guernsey and shortly before the Occupation began all but a dozen of the 1,800-strong population were evacuated to England. Alderney was the most heavily fortified of all the Channel Islands during the German Occupation (1940–45) because of its proximity to France. All the fortifications and the massive underground German network were built by slave labour exacted from the prisoners of war sent to Alderney. It has been estimated that as many as 16,000 prisoners of war passed through the island during that time. There were four prisoner of war camps on Alderney – Helgoland, Norderney, Borkum and Sylt – and a reception camp called Cittadella, which also held Moroccan prisoners. Helgoland, built on the Platte Saline, was almost exclusively for Russian and Ukrainian civilian prisoners, who were among the worst treated of the prisoners. Norderney, in the north-west of the island, close to the Mannez

Site of SS Camp Sylt, Alderney. Two men were crucified on the gates which hung from these posts. The author

Quarry where the old machinery left *in situ* makes it seem as though the prisoners of war stopped work just last week, held Belgian, French, Polish, Czech, Spanish and Chinese prisoners. Borkum housed German specialist workers, intelligent, skilled men who had objected to the excesses of the Third Reich and who were consequently forced to work for it.

Sylt, built in 1942 close to the airport, was the only concentration camp known to have been built on English soil. The 1,000 inmates were transferred there from Sachsenhausen Concentration Camp in Germany. From 1943 Sylt was run by the SS Totenkopfverband (Death's Head) Brigade and by all accounts it was a pretty hellish place in which to be incarcerated. Conditions were unspeakable, with a lack of warmth, sanitation and washing facilities; no medical care; acute dampness; infestations of lice; and rations below starvation level. In the winter of 1942 'breakfast was half a litre of black coffee without sugar; lunch was half a litre of thin vegetable soup; dinner the same plus one sixth of a kilo (about 6oz) of dry bread' (Charles Cruickshank, *The German Occupation of the Channel Islands*, 1975). Some starving Russian prisoners stole a lamb to eat and their punishment was severe: 'four men . . . [were] kicked and pushed around . . . the SS

Crucifixion on Alderney, 'Island of Death'. Illustration: Hannah Niblet

sergeant . . . went into the guardroom . . . to get a whip . . . made of woven leather thongs . . . indicating to the SS men that they were to fasten the four prisoners to the barbed wire with handcuffs, their hands above their head . . . their feet remained unfettered . . . after the prisoners had been handcuffed at the gate, they were whipped'. Beatings were frequent, especially of those who reported sick, and bloodhounds were used to drive prisoners over the camp boundaries who were then shot as escapees. Two men were crucified alive, one for stealing, the other for trying to escape: 'I saw one man crucified for stealing; he was hung . . . in the huts where the corpses were piled up . . . sometimes their lips, nose and ears had been eaten by rats' (interview with Ivan Kalganov, Russian prisoner of war: Madeleine Bunting, *A Model Occupation*). 'In a day or two we saw a crucified man on the gates of the [Sylt] Camp . . . it was Abdullah, killed for his second attempt to escape . . . when he escaped . . . he just went and sat on the rocks on the sea-shore . . . he was captured there and . . . made no resistance' (interview with Georgi Kondakov, Russian prisoner of war: Brian Bonnard, *Island of Dread*, p. 81; see also Peter Tabb, *A Peculiar Occupation*, p. 125).

When it became obvious that the tide of the war had turned in favour of the Allies, Sylt camp and most of its records were destroyed by the Nazis in 1944. The fate of many who were incarcerated within the camp walls is not certain, but it is known that nearly a third of Sylt's 1,000 inmates died between March 1943 (when the SS first took over the running of the camp) and mid-

June 1943. During the war, prisoners and soldiers alike had commented on the absence of birdsong in the area of Sylt. Even now there is still no birdsong to be heard. Today the camp site is overgrown and dangerous, with collapsed bunkers and unfenced machinery holdings. The Nazi quarters and canteen, which lay just inside the gates, are completely destroyed, and the subterranean building marked 'dance hall' seems a mockery. Almost nothing has survived above ground, except, bizarrely, the gateposts where Abdullah and his comrade were crucified.

After the war a report was commissioned by the British Government about what had happened on Alderney during the German Occupation. Captain Theodore Pantcheff, the investigating officer, concluded that 389 prisoner-of-war slave workers had died and had been buried on the island but even he had to admit that this was 'a minimum conclusion'. Survivors of the camps say that the true death toll reached thousands. They were the ones who were there at the time. They were the ones who suffered, who saw their friends suffer, who saw their comrades shot or pushed over the cliffs. They were the ones forced to dispose of the bodies from the camps – lorry-loads of them tipped into the harbour, until a new German Feldkommandant complained that the sight of all the corpses floating in Braye Harbour offended his sensibilities. The most searing account comes from a Spanish slave labourer ordered to dive down into Braye Harbour to retrieve an anti-submarine boom: 'a fantastic picture presented itself . . . among the rocks and seaweed; there were skeletons all over the place . . . crabs and lobsters were having a feast on the bodies which remained intact'. (See John Dalmau, *Slave Worker;* Peter Tabb, *A Peculiar Occupation*, pp. 125–6; Madeleine Bunting, *A Model Occupation*, p. 289.)

On windswept Longis Common, close to the site of an Iron Age pottery (now partially covered by a golf course) and an ancient nunnery standing by the shore, there was a Russian cemetery hidden in the tufty grass where forty-five Russians were buried in re-usable wooden coffins. The Germans, conscious as ever of external appearances, had even invited a priest of the Russian Orthodox Church to be present at some of the funeral services for the dead Russians. The remains of these unfortunate prisoners of war, who were beaten, starved or worked to death, have now been disinterred from 'this corner of some foreign land' and either taken back to Russia or buried in a Russian cemetery in France. There is also a memorial to the Russian dead in the graveyard of the gloomy cathedral church in St Anne. Other nationalities were interred in the Strangers' Cemetery (about a kilometre from St

Site of Norderney Camp, Alderney, and the former central Jewish compound. The author

Anne) until it became full. Adjoining what is now the former Strangers' Cemetery, the eighteenth-century Cemetery de St Michel has the German graves of those of the occupying forces who died on the island with a memorial to their fallen comrades – a stark reminder that in death everyone is equal.

To be attacked by the enemy forces was one thing, but Alderney was also attacked by an enemy from within and that was the worst of all. Of course Guernsey knew that Alderney had been almost totally evacuated a few days before the Germans invaded. After the population had left (somewhat hurriedly due to a lack of proper planning by the authorities in both England and Guernsey), it was perfectly proper and neighbourly that boats from Guernsey should come and take off the abandoned livestock to prevent the animals from dying or falling into German hands. It was also perfectly proper and neighbourly that household effects and items of value should be removed for safe-keeping until their owners returned. What was not perfectly proper and neighbourly was what actually happened: 'one of the Guernsey rescue parties which went to Alderney came back with rather more than the authorities had expected: clothes, furniture and food were dumped in the empty pool at La Vallette by St Peter Port for everyone to take their pick . . . one man returned . . . with

Hammond War Memorial, Alderney, commemorating the death of thousands of slave labourers. The author

loot including seventy-six curtains and thirteen clocks' (Madeleine Bunting, *A Model Occupation*). The pillaging and looting continued, and the Germans, initially conscious that they were to make the occupation of the Channel Islands a 'model occupation' as ordered by the Führer, notified the Guernsey police and left them to deal with the problem. Subsequently over a dozen people were arrested and seven were found guilty and punished by the Royal Court. When the Alderney population returned after the war, many families discovered that they had lost everything, and for the most part reparation was never made. So far as is known, the Guernseymen did not actually kill anyone on Alderney, but they did succeed in killing much of the trust and friendship between the two islands.

Today the Bailiwick still seems to be in denial about what really happened on Alderney during those dark days of war. There is little commemoration on either Guernsey or Alderney of the slave workers and the prisoners of war who died so wretchedly, no commemoration, and virtually no records of what actually happened. Guernsey islanders are understandably reluctant to talk or to share information. Alderney islanders were absent during the war and therefore have no memories of what happened on their island. The British Government did not bring a single German to trial charged with war crimes on Alderney, so that there is little information available in the public domain. In fact until this story was written, many Alderney islanders did not even know that their wartime archival records had been embargoed for a hundred years without explanation by HM Government. Their initial reaction was one of hurt bewilderment followed by anger that they are not allowed to know what happened to their island home in the years they were forced to be away. During the 1980s the Hammond family built a private memorial to the war dead of Alderney near Longis Common and each country which lost citizens on the island contributed a memorial plaque to 'those who also served'. Until 2045, when the truth may finally be known, it seems that Alderney will have to be content with this single simple gesture.

CHAPTER 26

Scandal, Intrigue and Poltroonery!

1785–95

'. . . he took a knife to the Royal Court and, seizing hold of Jurat de Havilland, threatened to have him thrown into Castle Cornet . . .'

A splendid and beautiful eighteenth-century château, a famous actress, a duel, a whiff of scandal: all essential ingredients of a good tale of dastardly deeds. Sausmarez Manor stands in St Martins on Guernsey. Seen from the road, the manor is imposing, built in the style of a typical Queen Anne house, three storeys high with attics and a roof lookout, so that early warning could be given of de Sausmarez family members returning home from the sea. Behind the façade to one side is a much earlier medieval stonework building. To the rear are the old stables, a vinery, and a large lake which is home to over a hundred ducks. Prehistoric remains stand in the grounds and an ancient trackway, said to be haunted by a spectral black dog, runs through the estate. It has been home to the de Sausmarez family for centuries, one of the oldest families on Guernsey. A late eighteenth-century de Sausmarez, Thomas de Sausmarez, Comptroller of Guernsey, married Catherine de Havilland, great-great-great-aunt of the renowned Hollywood actress Olivia de Havilland, who made her name in the film *Gone with the Wind* and is still best known for playing Melanie Wilkes opposite Vivien Leigh's Scarlett O'Hara and Clark Gable's Rhett Butler. Sir Peter de Havilland, Catherine's father and Olivia's great-great-great-grandfather, was Bailiff of Guernsey from 1810 to 1821, and he is the hero of this story.

Sir Peter was born in 1747 and educated at Caen in France. He became an advocate of the Guernsey Royal Court in 1770, the same year that William Le Marchant became Bailiff. The two men did not get on well and Sir Peter was upset when Le Marchant appointed his own son, Hirzel, as Procureur of Guernsey, and his young nephew, Thomas de Sausmarez, as Comptroller in 1774, a post that Sir Peter himself had hoped to obtain. The following year the two men clashed violently when the Bailiff suspended de Havilland's right to appear before the Royal Court because of his 'insolent behaviour towards the Chief Magistrate in the Royal Court'. The twelve Jurats decided that this was going too far and refused to try any more cases until the ban on de Havilland was lifted. The Privy Council complied, while bitterly criticizing the Jurats' action. Consequently all the Jurats resigned as a body. They were subsequently all re-elected by the States of Election but the Bailiff refused to swear them in. Again the Privy Council stepped in and he was ordered to do so, but four of the Jurats refused to be sworn in. The situation was fast becoming an impossible farce.

In 1785 when de Havilland was elected a Jurat he sat on the same bench as Le Marchant. This was altogether too much for the Bailiff, who accused de Havilland of perjuring himself in an affidavit he had sent to the Privy Council. De Havilland sued him. Bailiff Le Marchant was outraged. He tried to get the case thrown out. When that failed he took a knife to the Royal Court and, seizing hold of Jurat de Havilland, threatened to have him thrown into Castle Cornet and imprisoned. De Havilland was not cowed and pressed his suit. The Bailiff was incandescent with rage and now openly tried to influence the judgment. It says much that Le Marchant was actually allowed to remain as Bailiff of Guernsey after trying to pervert the course of justice, intimidating witnesses and making threats with intent to do bodily harm.

The Royal Court, Guernsey. The author

De Havilland won his case. He was awarded damages and, ironically, the Bailiff himself was sentenced to fifteen days' imprisonment in Castle Cornet. Le Marchant refused to pay. The Prevot of Guernsey, who happened to be Sir Peter's brother, Martin de Havilland, called at Le Marchant's home and told him that some of his property would be seized if he defaulted on payment. Le Marchant's response was to hit Martin de Havilland over the head with his walking cane and throw him out of his house. He was lucky not to be sued again by a member of the de Havilland family, but Martin de Havilland decided to take the matter no further. Perhaps he felt that Le Marchant had been sufficiently humiliated.

The Bailiff could not come to terms with de Havilland's victory, however. It was the first time that his power and prestige had not got him his own way and he may have begun to sense that at last the tide was turning against him for abusing the privileges of his office. He knew that there was much resentment against him for placing his own family members in coveted positions which, at least on some occasions, should have rightfully gone to others. Several of Le Marchant's contemporaries recognized that the de Havilland case had marked a turning point for him and they were not surprised when he eventually resigned the office of Bailiff in favour of his son Robert.

Sir Peter was also at loggerheads with Thomas de Sausmarez, whom Le Marchant had appointed Comptroller of Guernsey, and during a sitting of the Royal Court in 1790 they had a very public row. As a result de Sausmarez was told by Bailiff William Le Marchant that 'he was talking nonsense'; he was told by Hirzel Le Marchant that 'he was impertinent'; and by Jurat Robert Le Marchant that 'his plea was a tissue of nonsense'. The whole Court then became embroiled in a full-scale row with 'accusations and cross-accusations of cowardice and poltroonery', at which point Robert Le Marchant challenged Thomas de Sausmarez to a duel.

As the challenged party, Thomas de Sausmarez had the choice of weapon. Knowing that the Le Marchants had recently been practising with pistols, de Sausmarez chose swords as the weapons. They met at dawn the next day at L'Hyvreuse. De Sausmarez won easily but spared Le Marchant's life. Robert Le Marchant repaid him by putting up notices all over St Peter Port condemning him as 'a base lyar and a coward'. Naturally de Sausmarez sued. The case took three years to go through the courts but finally Robert Le Marchant was ordered to pay damages to de Sausmarez and withdraw his offending remarks.

Thomas de Sausmarez went on to settle down at Sausmarez Manor, marry twice and have a total of twenty-eight children by his two wives. The Bailiff, William Le Marchant, meantime saw to it that de Havilland's career as an advocate was ruined by nearly always giving judgment against his clients.

However, before he became Bailiff, Robert Le Marchant struck a secret deal with Sir Peter de Havilland. Robert would hold the office for ten years and then resign in favour of de Havilland. Obviously he too believed that his father had become obsessed with his hatred of de Havilland. Robert Le Marchant kept his word and resigned in 1810 and Sir Peter de Havilland took over the office of Bailiff, which he held until he died in 1821. William Le Marchant had died in 1809 and therefore did not live to see his hated rival assume the prized office of Bailiff. Peter de Havilland received a knighthood in 1817 for his services to Guernsey and because of his support for the military roads built by Sir John Doyle, which had caused much controversy. The main opposition to the military roads had of course come from the Le Marchant family; but although Bailiff William Le Marchant had initially won the battle, he ultimately lost the war.

Chapter 27

Murders and Mysteries of Lihou

1304

'Fifteen human skeletons were discovered . . . including a child . . . and three had brooches in their pelvic area . . .'

Lihou is a small rocky island of mystery and romance, offering beauty, peace and tranquillity; a place of pilgrimage to a priory which was the perfect religious retreat, looking out across the waters of Rocquaine Bay; so near and yet so far. On a summer's day with sunlight glinting on the rippling waves and the causeway between the island and Guernsey uncovered at low tide, the little island lies ten minutes' walk away, welcoming, beckoning. On a dark stormy night with a 20-foot-deep high tide raging across the causeway, it is one of the loneliest places in the Channel Islands.

The priory was founded by the Benedictine Abbey of Mont-St-Michel around 1114 and built on the site of an old pagan shrine. The chapel had a nave measuring roughly 10 metres by 7 metres and a choir about 10 metres by 6 metres. Caen stone was used to build the chancel arch and altar area and the floor around the altar was paved with green and buff tiles. A slate signed by someone named William Beauvoir and a large quantity of coinage dating from the mid-twelfth century have been found within the priory grounds. There were also two sundials made from Caen stone. A little way to the north of the chapel lay a large dovecote, and residential buildings stood on the site of the modern field centre, which faces the headland at the northern end of L'Erée Bay. An ancient roadway or 'chemin' ran across the island passing just north of the priory and led from the causeway to Lihoumel, a tiny island off the western coast of Lihou. By the fourteenth century Lihou had become a recognized place of Christian pilgrimage and passing fishermen lowered their topsails in recognition of Marie, Notre Dame de Lihou (the Virgin Mary), to whom the Priory church was dedicated.

Archaeological work on Lihou at the end of the twentieth

century revealed that the monks who lived on the island enjoyed a comfortable lifestyle by medieval standards. Discoveries include 'animal and fish bones that indicate a healthy diet, as well as an old walled garden, where they would grow fruit and vegetables, and shards of wine jugs from Bourdeaux and Rouen have also been excavated' (Heather Sebire, BBC 2, *Meet the Ancestors*, 1998). A stone mortar for grinding food and a green glazed serving dish are among other finds. Medieval cookery tended to mix meat and fruits, to keep vegetables separate, and to produce highly coloured foods (by using natural food dyes). Flowers and herbs were used for salads, and rose petals (safe to eat when washed but with a rather bland taste) were widely used as decoration. It sounds idyllic, but the treacherous serpents of murder and mystery lay in wait to disturb the peace and tranquillity in this medieval garden of Eden.

There had long been rumours about just exactly what went on in the Priory on Lihou. The island was cut off for between half

Lihou priory church ruins. The remains of Notre Dame de Lihou at which the witches of Le Catioroc screamed abuse. The author

and two-thirds of every day, sometimes more. At one time there were also nuns in residence, and a large clear rock pool, at least twice the size of a modern swimming pool, which lies off the west coast of Lihou facing the tiny island of Lihoumel, was nick-named the Nuns' Pool. The witches of Guernsey, who met regularly at the prehistoric grave of Le Trepied on Le Catioroc nearby, screamed abuse and taunts at Marie de Lihou, to whom the Priory Church was dedicated. Stories were rife of the black arts being practised on the island and of secret meetings between one of the abbots and a local wizard. Then there was the comparatively lavish lifestyle enjoyed by the Lihou clerics. There was supposed to be an abbot with just one monk for company on the island but the sheer size of the dovecote alone belies this, and certainly there was a sizeable little community living there in the early fourteenth century.

However, as in any small isolated community, tensions simmered, and one hot summer's day in 1304 something happened which destroyed the peace and tranquillity of Lihou. Thomas le Rover, a servant of the Prior, killed one of the Lihou monks, Brother John de l'Espin, right there in the Priory. When the body of Brother John was discovered the Prior sent for the Bailiff, Ralph de Havilland, who at once came over to Lihou. Thomas le Rover had been quickly caught. In the small force of men which de Havilland brought with him was a former Bailiff of Guernsey named Ranulph de Gautier. When they tried to arrest Thomas le Rover, fighting broke out and le Rover, trying to defend himself, was killed by Ranulph de Gautier, who then fled to the ancient church of St Sampson (founded in 1111) and claimed sanctuary. The Prior of Lihou, Brother Calfridus, and the remaining monks then panicked, took to their boats and sailed with all speed to their mother church at Mont-St-Michel, leaving the two corpses sprawled in the Priory precincts.

The next day two local men, Richard Paysent and Johanna le Veylette, went to Lihou and discovered it to be deserted, with food lying half eaten and tasks left half done like on the *Marie Celeste*, and with two unburied corpses lying just as they had been left. Thoroughly scared, they hurried home and said nothing. However when Brother Calfridus finally returned their visit was discovered and they were fined for not having reported what they had found. The grim task of clearing up began and the bodies of Brother John and Thomas le Rover were finally removed and given a proper Christian burial. Lihou tried to return to some sort of normality but this was far from the end of the story.

Ranulph de Gautier eventually escaped from Guernsey and

Lihou priory ruins. Brother de L'Espin was murdered and Thomas Le Rover was killed here. The author

went to England, where he managed to obtain a letter of pardon from the king. He returned to his lands in the parish of Vale on the island, but he was not a popular man and a few years later he was imprisoned in Castle Cornet. One of the charges laid against him was his part in the death of Thomas le Rover. While in the Castle, Gautier was 'put to death by many divers tortures' at the hands of three men: Gautier de la Salle, William l'Ingenieur and the ironically named John Justice. The two latter men were pardoned for this crime but Gautier de la Salle was tried by the Bailiff, Peter le Marchant, and hanged in 1320. Thus had the Lihou murder claimed a total of four lives.

The motive for the murder of Brother John has never been established. Perhaps Brother John caught Thomas le Rover pilfering from the Priory or poaching rabbits. Maybe they had a row which got out of hand. Or did Thomas le Rover witness Brother John doing something which a man of the Church should not have been doing? However, almost seven hundred years after the untimely death of Brother John, discoveries were made which show medieval Lihou in a very different light and give some credence to the fact that there is always a grain of truth in folklore.

In 1999 the BBC programme *Meet the Ancestors* assisted in excavations at the Priory led by the States. What they found was unexpected and startling. Fifteen human skeletons were discovered buried there. Five of these, including a child, were interred beneath the nave. Of the remainder, three lay outside the walls (indicative of suicides) and two were buried in stone-lined cists. Three skeletons were excavated and all three had brooches in their pelvic area. The brooches had been placed there for a symbolic reason and such grave goods are not usually associated with Christian burials. In February 2000 one of the skeletons, nicknamed 'Mr Lihou' or 'the Monk of Lihou', was reconstructed, using similar techniques to those used to reconstruct Lindow Man, the 2,500-year-old sacrificial victim found in a Cheshire peat bog about twenty years before. 'The Monk of Lihou' was a tall man (6 foot 2, or 1.9 metres, in height), aged between twenty-five and forty years old, a good-looking Englishman who had died around 1250. He was suffering from syphilis. Small children and sufferers from sexual diseases are not the normal incumbents of dedicated monastic graveyards.

The presence of a child's body is eerie and unusual. There are rumours that there were nuns on Lihou as well as monks but it was not usual medieval practice to mix the sexes in religious establishments, so as to 'lead us [the monks] not into temptation'. There is also an epic poem about an incident which took place in October 1595 when a local rector found himself cut off on Lihou with half a dozen island girls. The writer of the poem named him the Prior of Lihou, and the girls he called the nuns of Lihou. Unlikely as it sounds, the rector was persuaded to bed all of them! However, worse still were the tales of the monks cavorting with local girls and, according to some, even with witches. Certainly the general conduct of the Priory inmates on Lihou seems not to have been very exemplary and in 1484 the Prior was charged with heresy by the Abbot of Mont-St-Michel.

This was not all. A small carved face on a piece of Caen stone, measuring some 13 centimetres high by 5 centimetres wide, was also discovered. It was pre-twelfth century and therefore predated the excavated graves. The little face was said to be 'very human' in appearance with something feminine about it, and the facial features bore some resemblance to La Gran'mère at St Martins. This suggested the possible existence of a mother-goddess cult on the island. The Celts, from nearby Brittany and across the Channel in England, worshipped a mother goddess and had a tradition of carving free-standing human heads and faces. This tradition survived into the twentieth century in the English counties of Derbyshire and West Yorkshire. The intriguing question is, what was the likeness of a pagan goddess doing in the middle of a Christian priory on this tiny and remote Channel Island?

Paganism and witchcraft are said to have long been associated with Lihou and devil-worship is supposed to take place at Le Catioroc not far from the island. There is, however, a good deal of confusion as to the meaning of these terms. Pagan simply means non-Christian, although the word usually implies something not quite nice. Witches belong to the religion of Wicca, based on the mother goddess and the agricultural fertility cycle revered by the Celts, who worshipped the feminine as the giver of life. Wiccans practise 'white magic' and believe in the 'rule of three', which basically means that if they do anything unpleasant to people, they will get it back three times over! Devil-worshippers pay homage to Satan and practise 'black magic', often for their own selfish or evil purposes, and this can involve the sacrifice of a live animal, or even on occasion a human being. Was this why the bones of a child lay under the nave?

Legends abound of witches dancing with the Devil, who took the form of a black goat-like creature, on Le Trepied, the megalithic tomb at Le Catioroc (near L'Erée), and screaming abuse at Notre Dame de Lihou. Cries of 'Que hou hou Marie de Lihou!' rang out every Friday night from the capstones of Le Trepied as the witches whirled in their frenzied dances, sometimes led by the Queen of Hell. Friday is alleged to be the witches' 'sabbath', though this must refer to practitioners of the 'black arts' because 'white witches' only have eight 'sabbats' a year: on the four 'quarter-days' (21 March, 21 June, 21 September and 21 December), and the four main Celtic festivals (Imbolc/Candlemas, Beltane/May Day, Lughnasadh/Harvest Thanksgiving, Samhain/Hallowe'en), which can fall on any day of the week.

Someone once raised the question of why a reasonable-sized priory should have been built here on such a small island, rather than a hermitage cell for a single monk. Undoubtedly the answer lay in the fact that the Church was making a statement aimed at those who had worshipped at Lihou's former pagan shrine and at those who mocked Lihou from across the water. Despite the stories, the scandals, the murders and the mysteries, Lihou did become a renowned place of Christian pilgrimage. The Priory itself did not survive the Dissolution of the Monasteries in 1536 by Henry VIII, but its reputation survived the destructions of those times. In 1656 Dr Peter Heylin recorded in his *Survey of Guernsey* that while 'little more than the priory's steeple remained . . . those sailing past struck their topsails . . . such a religious opinion have they harboured of the place that, though the saint be gone, the walls shall yet be honoured'.

CHAPTER 28

Pictures on a Gravestone

1808

'. . . there without mercy [he] committed murder on the person of Olimpe Mahy . . .'

Until 1806 the main island of Guernsey was divided into two islands and the northern part of the present island, the Clos du Valle, was separated at high water by the sea running through from Grand Havre to St Sampson Bridge. Even today, two hundred years later, the path of the original tidal channel, the Braye, from coast to coast is still fairly easily discernible to the naked eye, although the Vale Pond is all that remains of it. There were two crossing places of the channel at the western end: one just below Vale Church (formerly an Abbey Church), known as Pont St Michel (after the saint to whom the church is dedicated), and one not far away called Pont Allaire; and in addition a crossing at Pont Colliche near the Bailloterie and one on the present Route du Braye near the Tertre. Vale Castle in St Sampson was built to protect this smaller island.

Today the northern part of the island is simply known as Vale. It is relatively flat and the northern coast is covered by sand dunes which conceal some of the oldest habitational remains, burial sites and ritual features in Western Europe. Les Fouaillages at L'Ancresse dates back to nearly 5000 BC. This end of the island has a completely different 'feel' to the rest of the island, peaceful, reflective, cut-off, with echoes of earlier times despite the volume of fast-flowing traffic on some roads and the crowds of Pembroke. It is easy to understand why the medieval monks chose the site of Vale Church to build their abbey.

In 1789 the French Revolution caused great alarm about the possibility of invasion from France, the more so by 1799 when Napoleon was in power. Fifteen coastal defence towers and a number of powder magazines had been built between 1775 and 1790 after the Seven Years War with France. To these were added sixteen forts or barracks and fifty-eight coastal batteries during the years 1789–1814, and by the time of Waterloo in 1815 a number of signal stations had also been built. Such military activity required the presence of large number of the militia, and several regiments were sent to Guernsey. They were not always pleased to be on the island nor were they particularly welcomed by the islanders. In 1783 there was a mutiny by an Irish regiment stationed at Fort George. Russian troops stationed at Delancey Barracks in 1799 indulged in drinking, stealing and rioting. One Russian soldier was caught stealing apples from an orchard at Duveaux Farm in St Sampson. The farmer shot the soldier in the legs, intending only to wound him, but in fact succeeded in killing him. The farmer then fled Guernsey and emigrated to America, where it is said that he founded the still-large Guernsey colony in the USA. Many of the soldiery stationed in St Peter Port were simply bored and looking for diversions, and it was against this background that one unfortunate old lady found herself in the wrong place at the wrong time.

In 1808 it was barely two years since the reclamation of the tidal channel had permanently linked the Clos du Valle to the 'mainland' of Guernsey, making communications with the 'mainland' easier. Olimpe Mahy was a seventy-five-year-old widow. She came from one of the larger families on Guernsey. Her husband, Nicolas Henry, had died in May 1789, when she was only in her forties, and was buried in Vale Church. Olimpe had remained living in the parish and acted as housekeeper to Michel Perrin, who lived at La Cour (The Court) in the Clos du Valle.

Robert Wilson was twenty-seven and a native of London. He was a soldier with the Royal York Rangers, who were stationed on Guernsey. Robert was bored with island life and yearned for the excitements of London. French was still the official language of Guernsey, not English, which meant that Robert, like many others, experienced difficulties as he struggled to understand everything that was said to him. On the morning of Sunday, 15 May 1808 he was meant to be attending a service at L'Église du St Michel, the Church of St Michael, in Vale, but Robert was fed up, hard up, and in need of a break. Assuming that everyone would be at the morning service, which he wouldn't understand anyway, he decided that God would understand if he absented himself and went for a walk instead. Castle Cornet could be a grim place at times and he wanted to savour a bit of freedom. See what attractions Vale had to offer. Doubtless his superiors would censure him for going AWOL but how would they find out? He would be back to rejoin his comrades before the service was over. What authority didn't know it wouldn't grieve over.

Olimpe Mahy was a devout woman and she often sat with her Bible. As she got older she wasn't always able to go to all the church services that she would like. On the pleasant spring morning of 15 May she got up early, as was her custom, and sat by the open window, smelling the flowers and enjoying the sunshine, listening to the church bells ringing out for morning service. She knew that everyone would be going to church, especially the young ladies, as the Royal York Regiment was also attending. Lots of new people coming to church up here now, not like when she was young. No need to watch the tides any more, she reminded herself. She had decided that she would not go to morning service on this particular day. Olimpe didn't hold with all these foreigners attending and, besides, her legs weren't good at the moment. She decided that she would simply sit by the window and read her Bible and communicate with God in her own way.

The May sunshine and crisp morning air felt good on Robert's face as he walked around L'Ancresse Common. He had managed to slip away unseen and he knew he had a whole hour ahead of him before he needed to be back. Besides, he needed to think. His soldier's pay wasn't enough to cover the amount he liked to drink when he was off-duty or to buy trinkets for the pretty girls with whom he liked to keep company, and he was in debt. He'd known how to solve that problem back in London, and he had paid for it too, but it hadn't deterred him. In fact that was why he'd joined the regiment. Get away for a bit. Let things cool down a little. Now he needed money again and he wasn't sure how to get it out here. He sat down to rest for a few minutes, staring reflectively out towards the sea where the sunlight danced across the water full of promise. He got to his feet with a sigh and as he turned round he saw the answer to his problems facing him.

La Cour was a large solid house, well kept, with a decent garden. Whoever lived there was not short of money. Robert walked slowly towards the house, quietly assessing its potential and unobtrusively looking to see who was around. The place seemed deserted. If he had learned anything at all about this island it was that they all went to church on Sundays. He also knew that here no one ever locked their doors. It was a golden opportunity, though he would have to be quick if he was going to get back to the church before anyone noticed that he was missing. As he crept through the garden of La Cour, Robert thought the house definitely looked as though it would be worth taking a peek inside. He found a side door which was unlatched and he cautiously entered the house. He was not disappointed. Whoever owned this house had both taste and money. Quickly he began to fill his pockets with as much as he could carry without it being noticed. Then, helping himself to a bottle of port which stood on a sideboard, he left the house by the back door.

She startled him, sitting there by an open window. He wasn't expecting to see anyone, having assumed that they would all be in church. Stunned, he stood still for a moment. Why did she have to be there? As if sensing his presence, she began to turn her head. She mustn't see him, he thought, or all would be lost. He dropped the port; taking the razor he always carried from his pocket and, creeping up on her quickly and stealthily like a cat, he put his arm through the open window, grabbing her head in an armlock, pulling her helpless towards him as he cut her throat from ear to ear. Olimpe Mahy never even had time to scream.

Hastily Robert pulled off his bloodstained gloves and pushed them into his pocket. He wiped the razor on the grass which was still damp with dew on this side of the house and hurried back towards the church. They were just coming out and he could see the officers talking to the vicar. He slipped back in line, not really sure if he'd been missed or not. If anyone had noticed he'd just say he'd been standing somewhere else. His uniform didn't seem to be marked. There was nothing to connect him with that stupid old woman at La Cour. However, Robert Wilson had made one bad mistake. Coming as he did from England's capital city, he had underestimated what a small island Guernsey is. Everyone was talking about the murder. It transpired that he had been seen, wandering around near La Cour. Although the witnesses hadn't known who he was, he'd stood out in his soldier's uniform. His comrades, when questioned, had to admit that he'd not been with them in church. In fact no one had seen him in church. Then a search of the barracks revealed items stolen from La Cour. Robert Wilson was caught so quickly that less than a fortnight after his attack on Olimpe Mahy he was standing trial for her murder, and before another week had passed he had been executed for that crime.

The *Gazette de Guernsey* for Saturday 4 June stated that he had been charged with breaking and entering La Cour, the home of Michel Perrin, between seven and eight o'clock on the morning of Sunday 15 May, where 'on the evidence of the King's Officers' he stole money and goods, and 'there without mercy committed murder on the person of Olimpe Mahy . . . cutting her throat with a razor'. The trial was short and the verdict a foregone conclusion. Robert Wilson was sentenced to be hanged and his execution took place between ten and eleven in the morning on Friday 3 June. Robert was philosophical about it. The murder was by no means

The tombstone of Olimpe Mahy in the graveyard of St Michel du Vallé. The author

his first offence and he appeared to be quite unrepentant. Really it was her fault for being there. Why couldn't she have been in church with the rest of them? He smiled as the *Gazette* thundered its disapproval: 'this monster, had committed different crimes in England, where he served his sentence . . . under the name of Wood . . . has refused to listen to the exhortations of ministers of religion and finished his days full of the sentiments which characterize a real scoundrel'.

Olimpe Mahy was buried in Vale churchyard, quite close to the modern entrance of the church on its eastern side. Unusually, there is a carving on her gravestone depicting the manner of her murder, as well as her epitaph, which described in detail what had happened to her. The writing is in French, which was then the language of the Islands. It is still visible but very worn and it is not easy to read. However until the mid-twentieth century, the image of the little old lady sitting in her chair, an arm clutching a razor reaching menacingly through the open window towards her, was quite distinct, but time and 'acid rain' have done their work, and the image, along with her story, is quickly disappearing into history.

Bibliography

Ahier, Philippe. *Letters on the case of 'A Crying Evil'* (Guernsey Pamphlets, vol. IX, no. 7, 1901)
Anon. *Escape from Castle Cornet* (Guernsey Pamphlets, vol. I, no. 2, 1830)
Anon. *Explosion at Castle Cornet* (Guernsey Pamphlets, vol. I, no. 2, 1830)
Bonnard, Brian. *Island of Dread* (Guernsey Press, 1983)
Bonnard, Brian. *Out and About in Alderney* (Guernsey Press, 1995)
Bouverie, Fred W G. *The Eleventh Hour* (1854)
Bunting, Madeleine. *A Model Occupation* (Pimlico, 2004)
Cachemaille, J L V. *The Island of Sark* (1874; rev. Laura Hale 1928)
Calendar of State Papers Domestic Series 1654 (PRO)
Carey, Edith. *Channel Island Folklore* (Guernsey Pamphlets, vol. III, no. 2, 1909)
Cliff, Capt. W H. *Jethou: History, Flora, Fauna and Guide* (Guernsey Press, 1960)
Dalmau, John. *Slave Worker* (Jersey 1946/7)
DeGaris, Marie. *Folklore of Guernsey* (La Société Guernesiaise, 1986)
Eggert, Harald. *The Channel Islands* (Robert Hale, 1998)
Findlay, A G. *Channel Islands* (Guernsey Pamphlets, vol. VIII, no. 4, 1873)
Gazette de Guernsey 1808
Girard, Peter. *Guernsey* (Guernsey Press, 1986)
Guerin, Lieut. Col. T W M de. *Guernsey Society of Natural Science* (Guernsey Pamphlets, vol. XVIII, no. 1, 1921)
Guernsey Press (various dates 1900–14 and 1945)
Guernsey Star (various dates 1820–1914)
Guernsey State Archives (1942)
Hawkes, Ken. *Sark* (David & Charles, 1995 rev. edn)
Hugo, G W L J. *Guernsey As It Used To Be* (*c.*1875)
Johnston, Peter. *A Short History of Guernsey* (Guernsey Press, 1994)
Kalamis, Catherine. *Hidden Treasures of Herm* (Herm, 1996)
Lamprière, Raoul. *History of the Channel Islands* (Robert Hale, 1974)
Le Huray, C P. *The Queen's Channel Islands: the Bailiwick of Guernsey* (Hodder and Stoughton, 1952)
Lihou Priory (Transactions of La Société Guernesiaise, 1912)
Manchester Guardian. 'Report of an investigation into the murder of 1000–1200 Jews and Russians on Alderney' (19 May 1945)
Marr, James. *The History of Guernsey* (Guernsey Press, 1982)

McCulloch, Sir Edgar. *Guernsey Folklore* (*c.*1919)
Moullin, J E (ed.). *Guernsey Ways* (Guernsey Society and Guernsey Press *c.*1967)
Pantcheff, Captain T X F. *Alderney, Fortress Island: the Germans in Alderney* (Phillimore, 1981)
Redstone Guide to Guernsey (1848)
Sanders, Paul. *The British Channel Islands under German Occupation* (Société Jersiaise, 2005)
Tabb, Peter. *A Peculiar Occupation* (Ian Allan, 2005)
The Times. 'Report of an investigation into the murder of 1000–1200 Jews and Russians on Alderney' (19 May 1945)

Index